Mini-Books are designed to
inform and entertain you.

They cover a wide range of
subjects – from Yoga to Cat-Care:
from Dieting to Dressmaking:
from Cookery to Antiques.

Mini-Books are neat
Mini-Books are cheap
Mini-Books are exciting

COLLECTING VICTORIANA

is just one Mini-Book
from a choice of many.

Other Mini-Books by Guy Williams

THE HOMELOVER'S GUIDE TO
   ANTIQUES AND BRIC-A-BRAC
COLLECTING CHEAP CHINA AND GLASS
DESIGN GUIDE TO HOME DECORATING

Some further titles in the Mini-Book series

FLOWER ARRANGEMENT
BUYING FOR YOUR HOME
COLLECTING ENGLISH COINS 1837–1971
LOOKING AFTER YOUR DOG
LOOKING AFTER YOUR CAT
LOOKING AFTER YOUR CAGED BIRD
LOOKING AFTER YOUR TROPICAL AQUARIUM
GIVING PARTIES
INDOOR PLANTS
NO TIME TO COOK BOOK
FAVOURITE RECIPES
WOOLCRAFTS
WINTER GARDENS
PATIENCE CARD GAMES
HOME MOVIES

GUY R. WILLIAMS

COLLECTING VICTORIANA

Illustrated by the Author

A MINI-BOOK BY CORGI

COLLECTING VICTORIANA

A MINI-BOOK 552 76357 8

PRINTING HISTORY
Mini-Book Edition published 1970
Copyright © 1970 Guy R. Williams

Mini-Books are published by Transworld Publishers Ltd.,
Cavendish House, 57–59 Uxbridge Road, Ealing,
London W.5
Filmset in Photon Times 10 pt. by
Richard Clay (The Chaucer Press), Ltd., Bungay, Suffolk
Printed in Great Britain by
Fletcher & Son Ltd., Norwich, Norfolk

CONTENTS

CHAPTER ONE

COLLECTING VICTORIANA

Most of us enjoy collecting things for our home—principally in order to make it a richer and more satisfying place in which to live. We are limited only by the bounds of expense—eighteenth-century furniture from the workshops of Chippendale and Sheraton may be very attractive, but it changes hands at figures well beyond the range of a normal person's pocket money. Porcelain from the factories at Bow, Chelsea and Worcester can be collected, similarly, only by the fortunate few. Queen Anne and Georgian silver is not likely to be given away with the proverbial pound of tea. Nor are early paintings or prints of any quality.

But there is one field in which the 'average' home-builder can still operate, and operate profitably. More interest has been taken recently in the numerous small pieces produced during the nineteenth century that are usually referred to under the general and rather derogatory heading 'Victoriana'. Twenty years ago, these were being thrown out, burned, broken up or (just occasionally) sent off to jumble sales in the hope of raising a few pence for charity. Today they are more likely to be properly appreciated, and the better pieces that change hands may find honoured places in the more reputable antique shops. But prices generally are still not prohibitive. Collecting Victoriana is therefore a thoroughly enjoyable and worthwhile activity. This book is intended to indicate briefly the great range of cheap 'treasures' that may be encountered today.

CHAPTER TWO

THE VICTORIAN AGE

To appreciate fully the pieces of Victoriana we may decide to collect, we have to know something about the extraordinary age in which these extraordinary objects were produced.

This was (to see it properly in perspective) the first time in the history of mankind when the personal supremacy of the superlative craftsman was to be challenged by the virtually inexhaustible resources of the insensitive, impersonal machine. Understandably, few nineteenth-century designers were able to adjust themselves at such short notice to so fundamental a change in the creative processes of mankind. Intoxicated with the power and earning capacity bestowed on them by a succession of newly discovered industrial techniques, those responsible for controlling and exploiting the resources of the proliferating machines lost, temporarily, almost all respect for the essential qualities of the materials they were required to handle. In their understandable excitement, they gave all too little thought to the virtues of restraint, of elegance, and of suitability of surface that had been so widely appreciated in the previous century.

The pace-setters of the Victorian Age were, then, unprecedently vigorous, formidably inventive and (from an aesthetic point of view) almost wholly irresponsible. It is the unbridled ebullience that results directly from their strengths and from their weaknesses that we look for, therefore, and value most highly nowadays in the typical products of the great Victorian industrialists.

Like most vigorous and well-fed extroverts, the successful Victorian industrialist liked to show off. So during Queen Victoria's reign a series of great exhibitions were mounted in England. The catalogues of these exhibitions, which have survived, tell us almost as much about the specially contrived, over-ornamented and wholly impractical wares shown in those displays of industrial virtuosity as Thomas Chippendale's *The Gentleman and Cabinet Maker's Director* and George Hepplewhite's *The Cabinet-Maker and Upholsterer's Guide* tell us of the infinitely more gracious pieces of furniture and household equipment that were being produced by the greatest craftsmen in the country a little over a hundred years before.

Among the earliest of the exhibitions that are likely to be of some interest to the present-day collector of Victoriana are those held in Manchester during the winter of 1845–46, and in London and Birmingham in 1849.

At the Manchester show the centre of the not over-large exhibition room was wholly occupied by a stand devoted to the products of the Stoke-on-Trent firm of Copeland and Garrett. (Copeland and Garrett's factory at that time covered more than ten acres of ground and gave a livelihood, of a kind, to approximately one thousand people.) Among the attractive articles arranged on this stand were 'breakfast services, toilet services, and hundreds of other important objects, sold in masses, and exported in crates by the thousand . . . unsurpassed in Great Britain in excellence of material, form and ornamentation . . .' There was a varied assortment of ceramic slabs intended for use in fireplaces, as table tops and as door furnishings. Exhibited, too, were some fine examples of Copeland and Garrett's statuary porcelain or 'Parian Ware.' (To be described, in this little book, at page 54.)

The exhibitions held in London and Birmingham in 1849 helped to sustain the interest in 'artistic' manufactured goods aroused by the Manchester exhibition. Prominently featured at the London exhibition were the 'Art Manufactures' produced under the auspices of 'Felix Summerly' (a pseudonym, this, that concealed the identity of one, Henry Cole). Cole was a great innovator—he was one of the first 'middle-men' to take the step of commissioning well-known artists to design run-of-the-mill domestic goods.

'We rejoice,' said the *Art Union Magazine*, soon after his enterprise was first launched, 'that Felix Summerly has succeeded in inducing such men as Mulready, Maclise, Redgrave, Horsley, Townsend, Bell and others, to aid in a project pregnant with immensely beneficial results to British Manufactured Art. ... We understand that arrangements are being made to carry out this project upon a very extensive scale, and that ere long there will be few of the manufacturers of England who will not contribute to it in one form or another. ... We understand Her Majesty was pleased to become the purchaser of all the more important works of the series.'

The enterprise lasted for three years only, but pieces bearing the Summerly marks still turn up occasionally today and are eagerly snapped up by keen collectors of Victoriana.

The Great Exhibition held in Hyde Park two years later was one of the outstanding events of the nineteenth century.

Thomas de la Rue and Company's stand at the Great Exhibition
geometrical staircase. 'It requires the space of one flight only,
other. Adapted for confined places and particularly for public

of 1851. In the background can be seen Langley Banks' twin
buildings where show rooms are required.'

admitting persons to ascend and descend independently of each

'The history of the world, I venture to say,' wrote Henry Cole, who was one of its principal organisers, 'records no event comparable in its promotion of human industry, with that of the Great Exhibition of the Works of Industry of all Nations in 1851. A great people invited all civilised nations to a festival, to bring into comparison the works of human skill. It was carried out by its own private means; was self-supporting and independent of taxes and employment of slaves, which great works had exacted in ancient days. A prince of pre-eminent wisdom, of philosophic mind, sagacity, with power of generalship and great practical ability, placed himself at the head of the enterprise, and led it to triumphant success.'

Under the devoted sponsorship of Queen Victoria's husband, then, a great glass palace, that covered approximately nineteen acres of ground, was erected in the royal park. It did not go up without causing a hysterical storm of criticism and abuse. 'The whole of Hyde Park and, we will venture to predict, the whole of Kensington Gardens, will be turned into the bivouac of all the vagabonds of London so long as the Exhibition shall continue,' thundered *The Times*.

'It is the greatest trash, the greatest fraud, and the greatest imposition ever attempted to be palmed upon the people of this country,' roared Colonel Charles de L. Waldo Sibthorp, sixty-seven-year-old Member of Parliament for Lincoln, in the House of Commons. 'All the bad characters at present scattered over the country will be attracted to Hyde Park. . . . That being the case, I would advise persons residing near the Park to keep a sharp lookout after their silver forks and spoons and servant maids. . . .'

In spite of all the considerable opposition, the 'Crystal Palace' (as Joseph Paxton's blown-up conservatory came to be called, with respect and affection) was completed by 1st May in the year appointed for the Great Exhibition. The reception of goods had started as early as the 12th of that February. Half of the vast glass pavilion was to be devoted to the display of goods from abroad; half was reserved for the exhibition of British wares. Queen Victoria was a frequent and almost indefatigable visitor, and recorded her impressions, much to the enjoyment of present-day students, in her effusive *Journal*:

> 'May 7.... To the Exhibition, remaining there nearly 2 hours.... We ... went into the Sculpture Court, containing many fine pieces including some by Bell, Thornycroft, Foley, etc. After this to Mr. Pugin's mediaeval room, full of church ornaments, beautiful mantel-pieces etc. and lastly through a collection of furniture, lamps, ornaments of the most novel and tasteful kind from Birmingham ...' 'Every time one returns to the Exhibition, one is filled with fresh admiration of its vastness, and never tires of it and its beautiful interesting contents ...'

And how varied and exotic those contents were! No serious collector of Victoriana should fail to study carefully the fulsome records that have survived of the greatest Trade Show of all time. Among the most extraordinary exhibits were:

> A sportsman's knife that comprised eighty different blades and instruments.
> 'A scent fountain, a jet for cooling and perfuming

apartments, etc.; kept in motion by a descending weight, and wound up like a carcel lamp.'

A 'Day dreamer' easy chair, made of papier mâché by Messrs. Jennens and Bettridge. 'The chair is decorated at the top with two winged thoughts,' said the catalogue. To the present-day observer, these 'thoughts' resemble buxom young ladies.

'A shield in silver' copied by Messrs. Elkington and Mason from the original by Vechte, using the 'beautiful and perfect process, electro-galvanism, which is becoming so valuable a hand-maid both to the artist and the manufacturer' (the catalogue, again). The subject of the bas-reliefs on the shield was 'A Battle of the Amazons'.

A stove of polished iron plate, in the form of a knight in full armour on a base of cast iron.

An ornamental clock that took thirty-four years to make. The clock incorporated (among many other notable features) a moving panorama of day and night, a perpetual almanac, a belfry with ringers and a bird organ.

An enormous and richly carved bedstead in Zebra wood that earned this penetrating criticism: 'The bed looks more fitted for a corpse to lie in state on than for a place of repose: it is a congeries of parts without an object: the footboard is so high and solid that it shuts in the sleeper as in a prison, and completely impedes the free circulation of air.'

'Patent ventilating hats. The principle of ventilating these hats being to admit the air through a series of channels cut in thin cork, which is fastened to the leather lining, and a valve fixed in the top of the crown, which may be opened and shut at pleasure to allow the perspiration to escape.' (Again, from the *Official Catalogue*.)

'Registered Alarum Bedstead.' (This time, from *The Expositor*.) 'By means of a common alarum-clock hung at the head of the bed, and adjusted in the usual way to go off at the desired hour, the front legs of the bedstead, immediately the alarum ceases ringing, are made to fold underneath, and the sleeper, without any jerk or the slightest personal danger, is placed on his feet in the middle of the room, where, at the option of the possessor, a cold bath can be placed, if he is at all disposed, to ensure being rendered rapidly wide awake.'

There were, too, some entirely novel electro-plated and Britannia metal coffee and tea services; embossed porcelain vases; rich damasks and chintzes and other textiles; groups of objects in glass 'in the oriental manner'; vases of wax flowers and plants; jewellery 'in the medieval style'; and many other strange and fanciful exhibits that can be seen, now, to have set a cracking pace for all producers of collectable Victoriana. With so much to classify, it is hardly surprising that a few regrettable errors were made. 'A wigmaker wished to be placed among the Fine Arts,' recorded Henry Cole, 'and found himself in Animal Products, which made him indignant.'

*   *   *

After that, exhibitions of a similar type (though not ever quite so extensive) were held at frequent intervals in several of the great European capitals, and many of the novelties prepared specially for them quickly earned international renown. English porcelain and Parian ware were shown at the Paris Universal Exhibition in 1855, and large quantities of each were ordered for export. Another International

Exhibition was held in London in 1862, and this was followed by the Paris Exhibition of 1867, at which work by the Irish 'Belleek' Company attracted much attention, the Universal Exhibition held in Vienna in 1873 and another Paris Exhibition of 1878. Writing about the last of these, George Augustus Sala wrote in praise of the pieces shown by Messrs. Doulton and Wedgwood, and of the wares exhibited by the less illustrious firm of Brown-Westhead, Moore, who mounted 'some remarkably well executed vases and plaques, displaying rare beauty of form and brilliance of colour, and of a variety of quaintly designed flower-holders, in which birds and animals are felicitously introduced'. Flower-holders of this type are eagerly collected today.

Although most of the showpieces produced specially for the great Victorian 'Art and Industry' exhibitions were regarded as oddities, and almost invariably finished up in museums, art galleries or private collections, the more modest pieces intended to stimulate the normal domestic trade had a great influence on contemporary taste. A quick look through Mrs. Isabella Beeton's *Book of Household Management* (quoted from in these pages) will show how lavishly the comfortably off Victorian housewife was expected to furnish her home, so that a suitably rich and ornate background would be provided for her frequent displays of hospitality. Many of the dishes and other utensils she purchased with such prodigality can be acquired, now, for relatively small sums, in second-hand goods shops and street markets. One just has to know what one is looking for!

CHAPTER THREE

COLLECTING VICTORIAN FURNITURE

Since the end of the Second World War Victorian furniture has been treated with more serious attention. Pieces that were once regarded as heavy, over-ornate and tasteless are now called solid, decorative and well made. Though prices are rising steadily, it is still possible to buy furniture made in the late nineteenth century for less than one may have to pay for pieces made in the last decade. And they will perform the same functions. If you are interested in collecting Victoriana at all you will probably wish to acquire one or two good examples of the Victorian cabinet-maker's craftsmanship, even though you may not wish to have so many that they give your home a 'Dickensian' atmosphere.

Victorian Furniture for the Sitting-room. The sitting-room, drawing-room or lounge (all these names are still heard occasionally) is primarily a place in which to relax. We will normally choose, then, to have the most comfortable seats we can afford, and only very rarely will our 'usual' chairs and settees be as much as a century old. But there is space in most sitting-rooms for one or two chairs that are only intended to be used occasionally. The collector of Victoriana will probably wish these to be Victorian chairs and he (or she) will have chairs of these well-known types to look for:

Tub Chairs. Only a fraction as expensive as the William

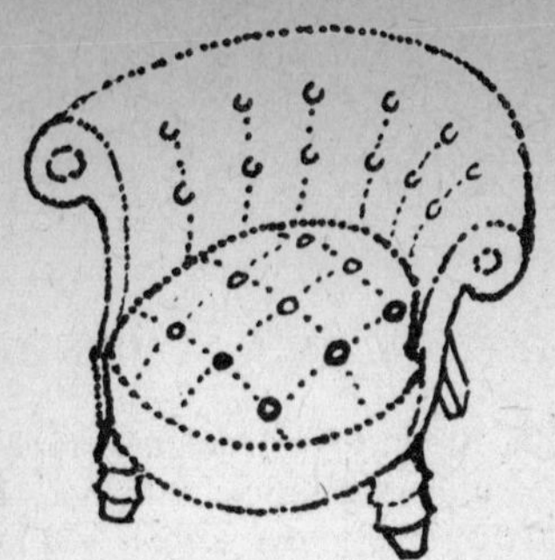

A Victorian 'Tub Chair'.

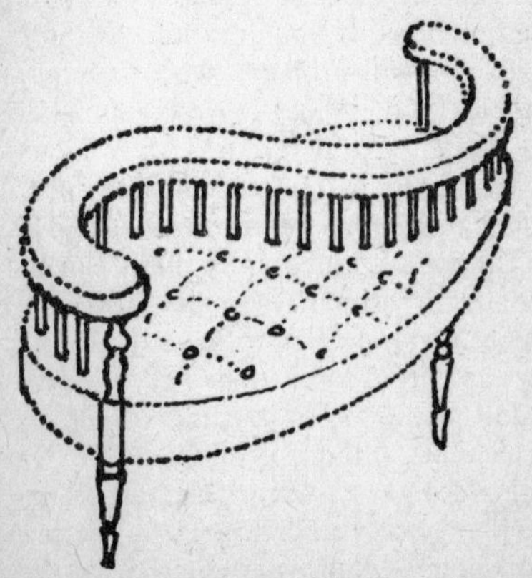

A Victorian 'Companion Chair'.

and Mary wing chairs, of which they are distant relatives, these squat, walnut-legged chairs were—to use Sheraton's words—'both easy and warm'.

Companion Chairs. Sometimes known as 'Natter Seats', these chairs accommodated two people, each facing the opposite way to the other.

A Victorian 'balloon-back' chair.

Balloon-back Chairs. At the beginning of Queen Victoria's reign this type of chair was just being developed from the type popular during the Regency, which had a wide horizontal yoke-bar that extended beyond the plain curved uprights. By 1860 balloon-back chairs were being made and marketed by the thousand, those intended for the dining-room being relatively plain, those meant for drawing-room or boudoir use being given some extra distinction with carved enrichments.

Vesper Chairs. This type of chair, also developed during the early part of Queen Victoria's reign, is sometimes known as a 'devotional' or 'prie-dieu' chair. A chair of this kind has a high back and a low seat, with very short legs. Sometimes vesper chairs are found that are most attractively upholstered and covered with Berlin wool-work (see page 96).

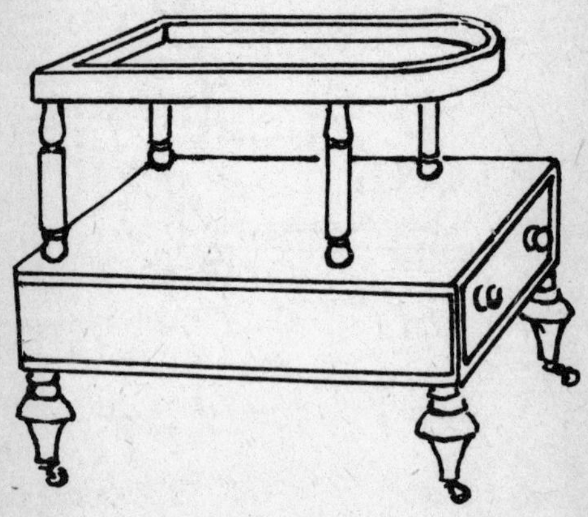

A Victorian supper canterbury.

Victorian sofas—made, often, with pleasantly carved wooden frames—can be given a new and exciting lease of life by being re-upholstered.

Genuine Canterburies—small wheeled trolleys made in Victorian times for holding sheet music—and supper

Canterburies (used, like modern dinner trolleys, for moving dishes and food) have been searched for assiduously by American collectors and their agents, and the prices of those that are left in this country have soared to such high levels that it has been found well worthwhile for reproductions to

A Victorian davenport.

be made in large numbers. Victorian 'Davenports' (small writing-desks) have risen sharply in value, too, but 'what-nots' (sets of shelves made to fit into the corners of rooms) can still be picked up occasionally for a few shillings in small-town junk-shops.

Victorian Furniture for the Dining-room. Genuine eighteenth-century dining-tables are sought for as eagerly as are silver Georgian coffee-pots, but Victorian dining-

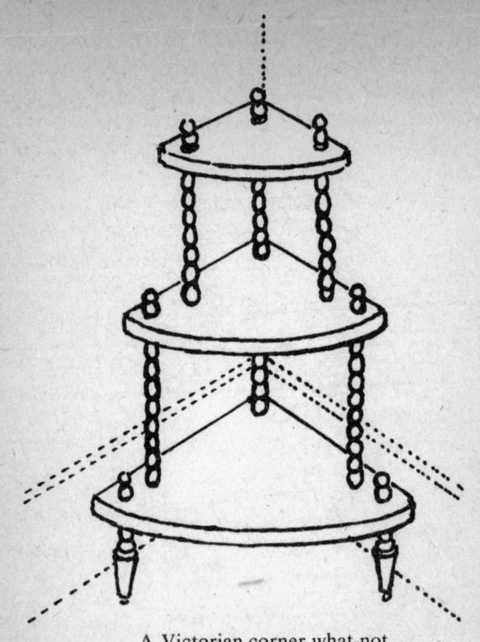

A Victorian corner what-not.

tables—massive, heavy and made, usually, by craftsmen who had no great respect for the work of Chippendale, Sheraton and Hepplewhite—are still regarded, by most collectors of antiques, as expendable curiosities. Looked at with an unprejudiced eye, however, these tables will often be found to be especially suitable to be incorporated in a modern 'mixed' scheme of decoration. The circular-topped tables known as 'Loo tables' (called that, after the Victorian card game, not after the smallest room in the house) were often made from, or surfaced with, exquisite woods, and are among the best buys in the second-hand furniture market today.

In all but the most cramped dining-rooms there will be space enough for a sideboard. Genuine eighteenth-century sideboards fetch three-figure prices when they change hands at auction. Victorian marble-topped sideboards and chiffoniers, regarded until recently as suitable sources of firewood, are not yet quite in the Christie's and Sotheby's class, but no one would now lightly pass them over.

There are other pieces of Victorian dining-room furniture, too, that should not be ignored. The revolving platforms placed in the centre of many dining-tables of the period (known sometimes as 'Lazy Susans') may be found

A useful Victorian table.

useful even today. Useful, too, are the various basket stands and wheeled trolleys on which the many plates and dishes needed for a lavish Victorian meal were transported or allowed to rest. Some splendid canteens of cutlery were made during this period, but those that have remained complete tend now to be rather expensive.

Victorian Furniture for the Bedroom. The Victorian period saw the introduction of the outsize wardrobe. These vast and heavy pieces of furniture are not always welcome today, even in homes with very large rooms, and they are quite out of place in the smaller rooms of the modern house or flat. The large dressing-tables and wash-stands associated with them are often disqualified, too, on account of their size. Nevertheless, they are often splendidly made, from choice woods, and they should not be turned down just because they are neither 'antique' nor 'modern'. When they can be purchased for reasonable sums they usually offer excellent value.

The brass bedstead, beloved by the Victorians and almost universally despised during the first half of this century, has bounced back into favour again with a vengeance—film stars and actresses earning thousands of pounds a week are proud, now, to be photographed against the knobbly heads of beds to which their mothers would not have given house room. Many of the brass bedsteads we see today are modern reproductions, but this does not necessarily make them less attractive to any but the most exacting collectors of Victoriana.

CHAPTER FOUR

BENTWOOD FURNITURE

In the years between the First and Second World Wars pieces of cheap 'bentwood' furniture were to be found in schools, offices, restaurants, church halls and other public places throughout the British Isles. They were entirely unappreciated, and all too often ended their days as firewood. Today the better kinds, with their graceful lines, have been found to sit happily in modern interiors, and chairs, tables and settees that could have been had almost for the asking a few years ago are now fetching surprisingly high prices.

Bentwood furniture was already attracting attention by 1851. One man seems to have been responsible for the foundation of the internationally successful bentwood furniture industry—it was Michael Thonet, who came from the delightful Rhineland town of Boppard, who first wondered whether a straight piece of wood could not be steamed until it was pliable enough to be formed into a geometric curve. His experiments proved that his ideas would work, and soon Prince Metternich invited him to go to Vienna to preside over a big factory from which pieces of bentwood furniture would be exported to many different parts of the world.

CHAPTER FIVE

PAPIER MÂCHÉ FURNITURE

Many early Victorian interiors contained one or more pieces of furniture that had been made from papier mâché. This material is surprisingly strong, and chairs and tables made from it were able to stand up to heavy weights without suffering any damage. Most of the finer pieces of papier mâché furniture are plainly marked with the makers' names—the firm of Jennens and Bettridge being responsible for some of the most attractive of the larger movable pieces; other firms, such as Dean and Benson of London and Waltons of Wolverhampton, tending to concentrate on the production of smaller decorative boxes and trays.

In 1825 Jennens and Bettridge took out a patent to protect a special process they had developed. By this process pieces of mother of pearl or pearl-shell were used for the decoration of papier mâché articles. In 1847 the same firm patented the process known as 'gem-inlaying'. They were able to use both processes in the decoration of the stained and painted wooden goods that are sometimes incorrectly labelled 'papier mâché'.

CHAPTER SIX

ELECTRO-PLATED GOODS

The beginning of the reign of Queen Victoria brought a discovery that was to cause much interest and excitement. From that time on, silver goods—or goods made apparently from silver—were to be produced at prices that brought them within the reach of all classes except for the very poor.

The successful development by Alessandro Volti in 1800 of a battery for the storage of electricity had made it possible for several inventors to experiment with 'electro-metallurgy'. Most of these experiments had failed when the layers of metal deposited electrolytically on some chosen base had simply failed to adhere. Exactly a year after Victoria succeeded to the throne, however, a patent was taken out by George Richards Elkington, in association with O. W. Barratt, that described an entirely new process for covering metals with zinc. It seems virtually certain that a single-cell electric battery was used in this process, though the patent does not say so in so many words. Elkington, who worked in partnership with his cousin Henry, was a prosperous manufacturer of small gold, gilt and silver articles, and it is fairly obvious that the cousins aimed, ultimately, to be able to cover cheap and easily saleable metal goods with thin layers of silver and gold.

By December 1839 Elkington was writing letters that show that he was ready to exploit a completely new plating technique. Helped by a Mr. John Wright, a surgeon from Birmingham, who had made some important discoveries, he had evolved a method of depositing by electrolytic means on a base fabricated from any suitable and easily worked cheap metal a perfectly even layer of silver of any desired thickness. And, he claimed, that layer of silver would remain securely in place in all normally foreseeable circumstances. Early in 1840 the Wright–Elkington process was demonstrated, and Elkington's claims were shown to be justified.

At first, owing to the relatively small size of the plating vats available, only very small articles could be plated electrolytically with silver——larger pieces, such as urns and tureens, were usually made from Sheffield Plate, and had only their smaller components (such as handles and spouts) made by the Wright–Elkington process. By the year of the Great Exhibition several manufacturing companies were working under licences granted by Messrs. Elkington, and were ready to show large and entirely electro-plated pieces in the displays of fine metalwork in Hyde Park. The Jury at the Exhibition were not over-impressed, recording their wish to 'guard against being considered as expressing an opinion on the merit of the application of the electro-process of silver plating to objects of domestic use. They desire only to commend the artistic application of this discovery, to which alone they are inclined to think it adapted.'

By 1861 there were no longer any such reservations:

'There is no limit to the art which may be employed in the production of plated goods by the new process of electro-deposit, and for articles in daily use it is now found to be quite durable as the old process. It now possesses this great advantage, that if after long use the

silver should be worn away in some prominent parts, the
article being composed of German silver or white metal,
the unsightliness of copper is avoided.'

Unlike the pieces made by the old Sheffield Plate method,
the new, electronically plated goods could be resilvered
without any difficulty when they became worn or scratched.

Victorian plated pieces can still be found and purchased
today in relatively large numbers, those made of 'E.P.N.S.'
(electro-plated nickel steel) being particularly easy to find.

CHAPTER SEVEN

VICTORIAN GLASS

Genuine eighteenth-century glass drinking vessels are now definitely expensive, but it is still possible to furnish one's shelves with attractive examples of Victorian glass for less than it would cost to buy a comparable number of modern pieces.

During the early years of Queen Victoria's reign glass factories in several different parts of Britain were producing clear lead crystal vessels in a wide variety of shapes and sizes. Many had 'cut' decoration of a type that had been popular since the beginning of the century (the heavy excise duties levied on glass had discouraged the few manufacturers who had shown any readiness at all to experiment). Wine-glasses cut deeply with diaper patterns of exactly arranged diamonds remained in fashion for several decades and are, in fact, still made and sold today. Early Victorian glasses of this kind can still be picked up for a very few shillings, and will probably prove to be an excellent investment.

Later in the great Queen's reign—that is, after the excise duties were removed in 1845—British glass-makers were able to experiment with the more florid styles popular on the Continent. Vessels made with coloured glass became especially popular. Even before the year 1846 was out, Benjamin Richardson's firm was able to mount at the

Manchester Industrial Exhibition a lavish display of coloured, opal and cased glass, and this inspired several other manufacturers to follow Messrs. Richardsons' example. At the Great Exhibition of 1851, where coloured pieces were shown by all the leading glass-workers, the firm of Rice Harris is recorded as having on their stand examples of 'opal, alabaster, turquoise, amber, canary, topaz, chrysoprase, pink, blue, light and dark ruby, brown, green, purple, etc. . . .'

As coloured glass came into fashion, cut glass of the type referred to above went temporarily out of favour (the great art critic John Ruskin, in one of his books published in 1853, declared categorically that 'all cut glass is barbaric'), and it did not return to popularity until the 1880s, when a special type of cut glass known, usually, as 'Brilliant' was produced for export to Sweden and America. This soon caught on in the home market, and by the end of Queen Victoria's reign large cut-glass bowls, vases and other pieces were to be found in places of honour in many opulently furnished homes.

'Cased' glass (referred to, above) was sufficiently popular in the nineteenth century for it to be worth, now, the serious attention of the collector of Victoriana. When a piece of cased glass was made a colourless glass vessel would usually be covered with one or more layers of coloured glass, which might be either clear or opaque. Then some patterns or pictures would be cut in the outer layer or layers, uncovering, where the cuts were made, the contrasting glass that lay beneath.

'Flashed' glass pieces may be as decorative as cased glass pieces, though they may not be quite as expensive. The process of manufacture was comparatively simple. After the glass vessel to be treated had cooled, it would be plunged into molten coloured glass and then removed, so that a thin layer of the coloured glass would be left on its outer surfaces. After that, designs could be cut in the coloured flashing to reveal, once again, the contrasting clear glass that lay beneath.

Engraved glass vessels are keenly sought by collectors, but as they can only be produced by craftsmen who are also artists and designers, they tend to be rather expensive. The designs—carried out, with diamonds, or with sharply pointed tools, or with small copper wheels used in conjunction with linseed oil and emery powder—included, in Victorian days, delightful arrangements of flowers, foliage, seeds, tendrils and other natural forms, as well as messages or pictures intended to commemorate royal weddings, famous victories, the openings of important buildings, bridges and railways, and other significant events. The Herberts of Dudley and the Woods of Stourbridge were Victorian glass engravers whose work is now very much admired.

The technique by which designs could be etched with hydrofluoric acid into the surface of glass was developed by the Swedish chemist Scheele during the eighteenth century, but it was not widely applied to domestic glassware until the post-Great Exhibition period. In 1865 an 'etching machine' was developed that made it easy for geometrical repeating patterns (such as the famous 'Greek key' pattern) to be etched by Scheele's method on the outer surfaces of wine-glasses and other suitable vessels. Victorian etched glasses can still be bought quite cheaply—odd glasses, left over from broken sets, may be, literally, almost given away. The delicacy of their decoration makes these under-valued glasses definitely worth collecting.

CHAPTER EIGHT

VICTORIAN MOULDED AND PRESSED GLASS

The early years of Queen Victoria's reign saw some revolutionary changes made in the glassware industry. Elementary glass-moulding techniques had been developed in earlier centuries, but it was not until the period in which we are principally interested that these techniques were applied to the production of domestic glass articles in a really wholesale way. When they were, a great number of useful and decorative household articles were made and marketed at prices that even the poor could afford. Plates, dishes, bowls, jugs, pin-trays, flower vases, salt, pepper and mustard pots, and drinking glasses of all kinds poured out from the factories in a bewildering profusion. Many of these early mass-produced glass pieces are extremely attractive, and can still be picked up for nominal sums—if, indeed, they are not still in everyday use.

The method of blowing glass into moulds was not so very different from the other age-old techniques of the craftsman in glass. The real, fundamental change came when some ingenious person (believed to be an American) saw how a 'follower' that corresponded exactly to the inside shape of the article to be produced could be used to press the molten glass into a mould that corresponded exactly to its outer shape. The distance between the mould and the follower would control exactly the thickness of the finished glass article at every point. This, it will be seen, gave the pressing process a definite advantage over the blowing process, since articles produced by the latter method tended to have glass of a fairly uniform thickness, and their inside surfaces were unlikely to be smooth. The pressing process was, too, much quicker.

Many of the most beautiful pieces of pressed glass made during Queen Victoria's reign came from the famous Ellison glass-works owned by Messrs. Sowerby of Gateshead. Sowerbys were at their most active around the year 1880, marketing new designs, then, with a fecundity that tends to confuse present-day collectors of their wares. (To take only one aspect of the matter, Sowerby's moulds were used for many years, and the colours of the goods produced from them in the later stages of their active lives were often quite unrecognisably different from the colours of the goods produced from them when they were first registered.) Collectors seek Sowerby pressed glass pieces in second-hand goods shops and stalls of the cheaper kind where their particular qualities are not likely to be highly valued.

CHAPTER NINE

VICTORIAN GLASS DECANTERS

No Victorian sideboard of any consequence was complete without a decanter to hold each of the wines and fortified drinks customarily consumed in the household. Today wines are rarely decanted (there is so little time, in our bustling days, for this leisurely proceeding), so the handsome vessels from which the Victorians poured their libations are only rarely collected to be used, and can therefore still be picked up for reasonable sums. Victorian decanters decorated with fine gilding may be a little more expensive, but they are, nevertheless, among the best bargains to be found today.

Cleaning Victorian decanters after use need present few problems. Just put a few small pebbles or pieces of coal inside, cover with a warm solution of detergent, and rotate gently. All stains and crusted sediment should be reasonably easily removed.

CHAPTER TEN

SLAGWARE

No serious collector of Victorian glass will remain unaware for long of slagware. This by-product of the Industrial Revolution, which sounds so unattractive when given that short name, is more happily labelled, occasionally, 'End-of-the-Day Ware' (the manufacturers were in the habit of purchasing the silicates that were drawn each evening off the surface of the molten iron at the neighbouring metal works, so that they could add them to their own transparent glass, producing an exciting variety of materials that might be almost as black as jet, or butter-yellow, or a mixture of colours). For more exclusive markets, slagware was usually labelled 'Vitro-porcelain'. There are plenty of slagware (or 'End-of-the-Day' or 'Vitro-porcelain' pieces) about, still—look for opaque, marbled boxes, bowls and vases—but their prices have started to rise.

CHAPTER ELEVEN

NAILSEA GLASS

No one can collect Victoriana for long without coming across the romantic name 'Nailsea'. Nailsea is, properly, a small town not far from Bristol at which coloured glass was produced during the greater part of the eighteenth and nineteenth centuries. Similar kinds of glass were produced, too, at Newcastle, Stourbridge, Sunderland, Warrington and other centres, but as it is usually difficult to identify the exact place of origin of any glass article of this period, the name 'Nailsea' is usually applied indiscriminately to all of them.

To appreciate Nailsea glass properly, one has to know that the factory there first grew to importance by supplying dark browny-green glass bottles for the Somerset cider trade. When the excise duties imposed on clear flint glass raised the price of domestic articles produced in it to levels that were almost prohibitive the glass-workers of Nailsea saw their opportunity and started to make similar articles in their own dark bottle-glass, on which only relatively low taxes had to be paid. As they increased their output and widened their range the Nailsea men became extraordinarily inventive, and evolved all kinds of new or more speedy techniques that would make their cheap wares seem more attractive without adding greatly to their cost. They learned —to take only a few instances—how to incorporate flecks of glass of other colours in a body of their own familiar browny-green; how to blow glass so that it had spiralling threads of colour in it; how to produce glass articles that had their smooth outer surfaces given an extra richness with raised ribs or quills; and how to form bumps or 'knops', in the act of blowing, that contained small trapped decorative bubbles of air.

Once the Nailsea workers had started to produce their new, inexpensive and extremely attractive goods in great quantities, it became clear that some of their most profitable opportunities for trade would lie in the mass production of cheap glass 'novelties' suitable to be sold as gifts, souvenirs and fairings. It is of these articles chiefly that the collector of Victoriana thinks when the name 'Nailsea' is mentioned.

Sometimes the word 'frigger' is attached to these ingenious glass articles by those writing rather romantically about the past. A frigger, properly, is a saleable piece produced by a glass-worker in his off-duty hours, but as industrial working hours in the nineteenth century were extremely long, anyway, it seems more than likely that only a very limited number of Nailsea pieces were actually made as 'foreigners'.

Among the Nailsea novelties looked for by collectors of Victoriana are:

Glass Rolling-pins. Sometimes these are found in attractive rich blue glass; sometimes, in striped glass; more often, in clear glass (made after the duty on flint glass was lifted) or in opaque glass with, perhaps, some gilded or transfer-printed motto, view or message. Occasionally a hollow glass rolling-pin will be found with its original contents (sweetmeats or some other small gifts) intact and unspoiled by the passage of time.

Glass Wish Balls, or 'Witch' Balls. Found, sometimes, in plain dark colours; sometimes, in the same kinds of glass enriched with flecks or spots; occasionally, even, bearing texts from the Bible inscribed in careful Victorian lettering.

Glass Flasks. These useful little containers, that may be mottled, striped, quilted or decorated in a number of other ways, turn up in an almost endless variety of shapes and sizes. Some of the most intriguing Nailsea flasks are made to represent small pairs of bellows—those used to coax a low fire into a blaze in Victorian times.

Glass Pipes. Smoking was not regarded as a respectable habit in all Victorian family circles. (In many homes there was a room specially set aside to which the gentlemen and their male guests could retire when they wished to enjoy the 'noxious weed'—as it was often called—without causing unnecessary annoyance to the members of the gentler sex. In the strictest households tobacco smoking could only be indulged in a clandestine way at the bottom of the garden.) The craftsmen of Nailsea and the other great Victorian glass-working centres seem to have enjoyed creating playful representations of the long-stemmed pipes that were fashionable at that time. These were decorative rather than useful, and, being fragile, have not always survived. Those that have are worth a little careful cherishing.

CHAPTER TWELVE

VICTORIAN PORCELAIN AND POTTERY

During the first three decades of Queen Victoria's reign British potteries were producing for home markets and for export an enormous variety of attractive and saleable wares. A fair proportion of these have survived intact, and the collection of nineteenth-century porcelain and pottery can be, in consequence, a highly rewarding pastime for the not-so-rich.

Transfer-printed earthenware became popular earlier in the nineteenth century, with 'willow pattern' and other designs executed in a single shade of blue. By the 1830s and 1840s new techniques had been developed that made it possible for designs and pictures to be printed on earthenware in a number of other colours—such as red, orange, yellow, green, brown and purple—the whole being protected, when the processes of decoration were complete, by a transparent, impermeable glaze. At the time it must have seemed as though most of the factories in the Midlands were fully occupied in this highly competitive industry.

Prominent among the leaders were Copelands. Alderman W. T. Copeland, who was later to be Lord Mayor of London, bought the business from the third Josiah Spode in 1833, and he continued to run it, in association with his partner and principal traveller, Thomas Garrett, until 1847.

In that year the partnership of 'Copeland and Garrett' was dissolved, and the name of the undertaking was changed to 'W. T. Copeland late Spode'. After 1867 the firm was known as 'W. T. Copeland and Sons'. Copelands were famous throughout the Victorian period for their magnificent dinner and tea services. They introduced new colours to the industry (their 'Sardinian green' and 'cerulean blue' being particularly popular), and they were among the first manufacturers to incorporate successfully Japanese motifs in their English designs. Odd Copeland plates and cups and saucers, decorated exquisitely with flowers, can still be picked up occasionally by the keen-eyed collector.

The great firm of Coalport was founded in 1750, and this date, with the letters 'A.D.', is, misleadingly, to be found stamped on many late Victorian pieces. Coalport specialised in the production of pieces made in the styles first used at Sèvres, many years before, and all collectors of Victorian porcelain will come across examples of the firm's work decorated with the well-loved tint 'Rose du Barry' or, as it was more correctly called, 'Rose Pompadour'. Coalport pieces decorated with fine paintings of birds, animals and flowers tend to fetch high prices today.

Worcester is a city from which porcelain pieces of fine quality continued to pour in some profusion throughout the Victorian era. At the beginning of the period there were three different porcelain factories in the city, but Flight, Barr and Barr amalgamated with Chamberlain and Co. in 1840, and the reorganised firm continued under the latter name. In 1852 a further reorganisation led to the firm being known for a time as 'Kerr and Binns', and in 1862 the company became the 'Worcester Royal Porcelain Works'. Graingers, the 'odd men out', were absorbed by the larger undertaking in 1889. Grainger pieces that demonstrate the firm's own special effect known as 'ceramic lace drapery' are well worth hunting for today.

Mintons, of Stoke-on-Trent, were working with great industry and brilliance during the Victorian era. One is not likely to find at a reasonable price any piece by their most famous designer, the Frenchman M. L. Solon, but pieces of great splendour made for more modest markets can still be purchased by collectors who are not yet in the millionaire class.

The porcelain produced during the Victorian period at the factories mentioned above, and at numerous smaller undertakings, demonstrates most effectively the desire of the home-makers of that era for sumptuous richness and comfort. Elaboration of design and intricacy of detail were prized above the simple elegance admired in the previous century. To help those who have a taste for the more exuberant Victorian work there are now some splendid works of reference. These are recommended in the Book List on page 127.

CHAPTER THIRTEEN

STAFFORDSHIRE FIGURES

Staffordshire figures have a long history. Some of the earliest—those produced in the villages of Burslem, Fenton, Hanley, Longport, Shelton and Stoke during the eighteenth century, for example, by the Adams, the Turners, the Wedgwoods and other families—now fetch very high prices when they change hands. Made, often, in small workshops associated with farms, so that the men who produced them would be able to milk the cows while their various batches of work were in the kilns, these primitive ornaments have the same rough vigour as the people who gave them their shape.

By the beginning of Queen Victoria's reign the production of pottery figures had expanded until their manufacture was one of the Midlands' most thriving industries. Different types of ornament were being produced to satisfy different types of customer. Very crude examples were being turned out by the thousand for the travelling pedlars of the time to take round to fairs and street markets:

> *My casts are formed to get my bread*
> *And humble shelter for my head*

was the distinctive cry of these itinerant 'image men'. More refined and expensive figures were being produced to appeal to the more sophisticated patrons who were used to seeing

the delightful porcelain pieces that had been produced at
Bow, Chelsea and Derby. There were few houses or cottages
in rural areas that did not have a row of these gaily coloured
ornaments on the chimney breast or mantelshelf.

Few collectors of Victoriana will be able to resist the
temptation to acquire a number of these homely and charming pieces. If they appeal to you, you will find that it is still
possible to obtain good examples for quite reasonable sums.
The enormous numbers in which many of the most attractive designs were produced prevents them from being
regarded as rarities. Here is a short review of the main
categories into which Staffordshire earthenware figures can
be roughly divided:

Portrait Figures. The 'flat-back' and 'all-round' figures
found on so many Victorian chimneypieces offered a portrait gallery of an extraordinary range. Members of the
royal families of the world, heroes and villains, actors and
actresses, singers, explorers, inventors—people of all these
types and many more were represented in varying degrees
of truthfulness, some of the portraits, carried out by the less
skilful workers, being distinctly unflattering. Cottage-
dwellers who lived before the days of the camera and the
illustrated newspaper would find them all exciting, however,
even the lumpiest caricatures, and they retain much of their
interest today.

Of prime importance as a subject for portrait figures was,
of course, Queen Victoria herself. (As a person known to be
encouraging the quieter domestic virtues, she was thought to
be especially fitted to preside over the family hearth.) So she
was represented in 'flat-back' and 'all-round' form at every
stage of her reign, from her accession as a shy and virtually
unknown young girl to the Diamond Jubilee held in 1897.

She is shown with and without her husband, Prince Albert; with and without her various children; sometimes with some foreign potentate such as the Sultan of Turkey; and occasionally with a dog. Prince Albert and the other members of the family were often shown, too, on their own and without the imperial matriarch. One of the most popular mantelpiece ornaments in the 1850s showed the Queen's two eldest children out for a ride in their pony cart.

Famous statesmen, too, were thought to be especially suitable for representation near the family hearth. (We can still find portraits of Sir Robert Peel, D'Israeli and Gladstone, today, on many cottage mantelshelves). The military and naval heroes who proved to be particularly popular were Nelson and the Duke of Wellington—portraits of these two men went on being made long after they were dead—and when the Afghan War of 1842 and the Crimean War of 1851–52 engaged the country's attention portraits of the commanders, principal officers and medal-winners were produced as rapidly as news could be brought from the battlefields. (Lord Raglan of the 'Gallant Six Hundred', Florence Nightingale and Piper Findlater, for instance, were quickly commemorated by the Staffordshire image trade.)

We can learn, too, from Staffordshire figures, much about the Victorians' attitude to famous people abroad. A specialised collection could be quite easily made of portraits of non-British subjects, and very interesting it would prove. Examples that spring to mind from the many available include the portraits of the American Presidents Abraham Lincoln and Benjamin Franklin; of Moody and Sankey, the Victorian predecessors of Billy Graham; and of Mrs. Bloomer, who first devised the article of female attire on which her name was so memorably bestowed. Prussians similarly honoured included King William I and Bismarck; among the Italians portrayed was Garibaldi (whose visit to England in 1864 caused much excitement). Shown, too, was Colonel Peard (1811–80), who helped Garibaldi in 1860 in the invasions of Sicily and Naples. Peard bore so remarkable a resemblance to the great Italian that he was frequently referred to as 'Garibaldi's Englishman'.

Portraits of well-known criminals have increased noticeably in value recently—possibly because they are being made the subject of an increasing number of specialised collections. Several of the most lurid murders of the time are commemorated by portraits of the killers (James Rush, of Potash Farm near Wymondham, who was hanged at Norwich in 1849 after having shot two men dead and wounded two women, was a favourite subject); by portraits of the victims (Maria Marten, murdered by William Corder in the Red Barn, can still be found in effigy in countless homes); and by representations of the buildings in or near which the crimes were committed. Struggles between gamekeepers and armed poachers also provided a favourite theme.

Animals. The British first became widely known as a nation of abnormally sentimental animal lovers during Queen Victoria's reign. It followed, then, that the potters of Staffordshire did not need any persuasion to cater fully for this popular taste. To collect pottery animals indiscriminately would be to lay oneself open to almost endless expenditure and, eventually, to being crowded out of one's home. Most collectors of Victoriana choose, therefore, to limit their purchases of Staffordshire animals to one particular kind.

Dogs are, of course, the most popular and the most

numerous of all. Sentimental Staffordshire spaniels, made in pairs so that one could sit at each end of a mantelshelf, were produced and sold in great quantities, those intended for the 'expensive' end of the trade being often decorated with gold chains and lockets and sometimes with flowers. Almost as popular were the whippets and greyhounds so widely used at that time for the well-loved pastime of coursing. Some of these representations of working dogs are relatively crude, and lack all the grace of the swift creatures on which they were based. Others are passably good portraits of individual dogs—the winners, perhaps, of important trophies. The hounds of both types are shown in a variety of attitudes and are often depicted with a hare or rabbit in the mouth. Also collected keenly are Staffordshire poodles, foxhounds and a variety of lap dogs.

Cats do not seem to have been nearly as popular as dogs—they are not found as frequently, even, as sheep, which are sometimes made the subjects of specialised collections. (One of the most elaborate and charming pieces in the author's possession shows a shepherd and shepherdess sitting on a grassy mound, shaded by a simple tree, surrounded by their flock.) Wild animals such as lions and elephants were also popular, the pairs of striped zebras which were so well liked in Victorian times being most useful as decorative features today. The catalogue could be extended almost indefinitely, but it will be better for the intending collector to study one of the authoritative works mentioned in the Book List on page 127.

Anyone collecting Staffordshire earthenware figures should know how these ornaments were made.

First, a clay model was made that corresponded as closely as possible to the shape intended for the finished ornament. Then 'master moulds' would be made with plaster of Paris from the clay prototype. From these master moulds, which were usually divided into a number of parts, a plaster replica of the original figure could be obtained, and from this replica more 'working moulds' could be made. These duplicated working moulds made it possible for great numbers of replicas to be produced for sale if the pattern proved popular.

Every 'flat-back' figure should be studied carefully for signs of individual workmanship. When long runs of any figure were called for it was usual for some parts to be added by skilled craftsmen to the parts produced repetitively by less skilled operatives from the mould. A horse taken from a simple mould, for instance, might be minus the two nearside legs. These legs would have to be individually modelled and added to the incomplete horse by a skilled workman before the clay could be fired in a kiln to the hard or 'biscuit' state. After this first, or biscuit, firing the under-glaze colours would be painted on, and then the figure would have to be fired again, so that these would be hardened.

Next, the figure would be dipped in a liquid glaze derived from lead, and then it would be fired again. At this stage the surface of the figure would be hard and non-porous.

Finally, the overglaze enamels would be brushed on to the figure wherever they were needed.

Not all the 'Victorian' Staffordshire earthenware figures you are offered will be genuinely old. Far from it. Many have been made in the present century from moulds that have been carefully preserved from the great days of the industry. A close study of the surface of a genuine nineteenth-century example will often reveal a fine network of tiny cracks, or 'crazing'. These were caused by the erratic way in which the earthenware and the glaze applied to it contracted during the firing. Modern glazes are usually more nearly perfect as a result of better temperature control. The colours used in the modern industrial processes tend, too, to be noticeably different from those available for colouring the original figures. It is a good idea to study closely a few indisputably genuine examples—those, say, in a reputable museum—before laying out a lot of money on doubtful wares.

CHAPTER FOURTEEN

LUSTRE WARE

Until the beginning of the nineteenth century only the rich could afford to have large, handsome gold and silver vessels in their homes. Then, in the early years of the century, 'lustre ware' was developed, and pots, bowls and jugs were produced—in small quantities—that had gleaming surfaces, and which looked as if they were made from one of the more precious metals. By the beginning of Queen Victoria's reign cheaper lustre goods were being produced in greater numbers, many of them for export to America. At the great exhibitions of 1851 and 1862 these goods were prominently displayed.

Lustre pieces fall into three fairly distinct categories. Gold lustre owes its colour and warmth to a thin coating of gold, applied in a solution. The lustre is not quite opaque, and it is liable, therefore, to be affected by the colour of the ground to which it is applied. If it is laid on a white or pale earthen ground the surface that results will usually have a faint but charming tinge of pink. If it is laid on a dark brown or chocolate-coloured ground the surface produced will be the warm rich gold referred to, usually, in the trade as 'Copper lustre'.

Silver lustre owes its brilliance to a thin coating of platinum, applied in solution. This lustre is more opaque than gold lustre, and some collectors think that it lacks much of the subtlety of the warmer wares.

Not all the examples of lustre ware to be seen in antique and second-hand goods shops today can be correctly included in a collection of Victoriana, for modern reproductions are being marketed by a number of firms. Genuine Sunderland ceramic wall plaques, which usually featured some pious message surrounded by a frame decorated with lustre, are rising rapidly in price, but attractive lustre jugs, admirably suited for floral arrangements, can still be picked up at fairly reasonable prices.

CHAPTER FIFTEEN

PARIAN WARE

Ever since classical times white marble has been admired throughout the Western World as being the material chosen by the greatest sculptors for much of their most memorable work. Unfortunately, marble has to be carved away laboriously by highly skilled hands before any sculpture can be made from it. Until Messrs. Copeland and Garrett of Stoke-on-Trent introduced their Parian Ware in the early days of Queen Victoria's reign, sculptures and statuary figures were regarded as appropriate ornaments for the homes of the wealthy, but impossibly expensive for the homes of the less well-to-do.

Messrs. Copelands' enterprise changed all that. Their 'Parian' figures could be mass produced. These figures were creamy white and gleaming, and looked like marble, but they were so much more easy to deal with, because they were made from a material that could be used in a liquid state. This material was technically termed 'slip', and was about the consistency of thick cream. It was poured into moulds that formed a figure or group (for the production of one single group, representing 'The Return from the Vintage', which consisted of seven figures, more than fifty moulds were required). The moulds were made of plaster, and rapidly absorbed much of the moisture from the slip. The coating next to the mould, then, formed a sufficiently thick skin to be cast, the superfluous slip being poured back into the mixing vessel. The material to be cast, that remained in the mould, would then be heated to a very high temperature, so that it became quite hard. After the various parts of a figure or group had been 'fired' in this way they would be removed from their moulds, cleaned up and assembled with a cement made of slip. Further firings would be required before the work was complete.

Other firms, such as Mintons and Wedgwoods, soon followed the example of Messrs. Copelands. (Some of them are believed to have been carrying out their own researches even before Copelands made their first announcement.) For their ware, Wedgwoods preferred to use the name 'Carrara' rather than 'Parian', probably because they thought that the place-name would remind people of the real marble that had, for centuries, been quarried there. Methods of colouring Parian products and of incorporating more refined detail were quickly discovered, and soon after a 'reducing machine' was devised by Benjamin Cheverton that made it possible for an exact small-scale replica to be produced of any statue or similar object, figures and groups 'in the Greek and Roman taste', reproductions of works by leading Academicians, pseudo-Classical ornaments and a wide variety of other attractive pieces. Soon they were being marketed at astonishingly reasonable prices.

The number of different Victorian Parian Ware pieces that can be picked up by observant collectors today is, still, sufficiently large to make this a most rewarding field of research. As soon as the first production difficulties had been successfully overcome, exhibitions and shops were kept supplied with Parian goods as massive as life-size reproductions of Grecian and Roman athletes and warriors, and as small as floral studs for the fronts of Victorian gentlemen's shirts. Some industrialists—as, for example, Mr. Potts, the 'eminent manufacturer of Birmingham'— made a feature in their lists of pieces that combined Parian Ware with various metals ('We have on several occasions advised the union of statuary porcelain with metal', claimed the *Art Union Magazine* in the 1840s, 'and it gives us much pleasure to see our suggestion very satisfactorily carried out. . . . The objects produced on this plan consist of flower vases, candle lamps and gas brackets . . . the metal is of brass, bronze, or electro silvered or gilt, the figures are of Copelands statuary porcelain. . . .')

Many famous people were represented in portrait form in Parian Ware (Shakespeare, Milton, Sir Robert Peel, Sir Walter Scott—a full list would seem almost endless) and so, too, were a number of people (Eve, Sappho and Lady Godiva, for example) whose exact appearance was entirely a matter of conjecture. Animals and birds were popular subjects. As many as a hundred different companies are believed to have produced and marketed, at various times, extensive ranges of goods in Parian Ware. Some continued to do so even after the end of the Victorian era.

CHAPTER SIXTEEN

POT LIDS

In the early years of the nineteenth century many delicacies (such as pastes and relishes) and toilet necessities and luxuries (such as pomatum and the bear grease that was used on gentlemens' hair) were packed in round earthenware pots, the lids of which were decorated with interesting and colourful pictures. The lids made in the earliest years of Queen Victoria's reign were generally decorated by hand, the artist being restricted to a small range of underglaze colours, or they were decorated in a single colour by the simple transfer-printing method favoured at that time.

In 1846 and 1847, however, the demand for new and attractively decorated pot lids increased, and patents were taken out for new and improved processes by which two or more coloured images could be applied to a single lid, producing a richer and more varied effect. On most pot lids made after this time, small spots or rings can be seen that were intended to act as locating points to guide the workers whose job it was to combine the various colour prints so that they registered correctly.

Sometimes you may hear the whole range of Victorian pot lids referred to rather carelessly as 'Prattware'. This name is loosely applied to these charming pictorial covers because the great firm of Messrs. F. and R. Pratt, of Fenton, Staffordshire, offered many of the most splendid designs, and were able, in their products, to achieve richer colouring and more subtle effects of light and shade than any found in the wares of their competitors.

The collector of Victorian pot lids has a very wide range of subjects to search for. He—or she—may find lids embellished with views of famous cities or rivers; with portraits of celebrities; with floral arrangements; with studies from natural history; with illustrations suggested by notable incidents in favourite books and plays; with pictures of topical events, such as the great international exhibitions referred to earlier in this book; with scenes from life in Old England; and with an almost endless variety of other designs. No one hoping to collect pot lids seriously can afford to be without a copy of Harold G. Clarke's *The Pictorial Pot Lid Book*, which was published in 1960.

Unfortunately for the collector of Victorian pot lids, this is a field in which the faker and forger have been especially active. Many of the copper plates from which Messrs. Pratt's designs were printed in the nineteenth century still exist. In the grey years of austerity that followed the Second World War they were used to produce 'reproductions' that could be offered for sale at prices that the ordinary home-lover could afford.

If you are at all doubtful about the authenticity of any pot lid you may be offered, look at it sideways, and examine its profile. Any pot lid that has a level top surface will probably be a twentieth-century reproduction. If it has holes in the side—made specially, so that it can be hung up—it is certain to be 'new'.

CHAPTER SEVENTEEN

PASTILLE BURNERS

For centuries it was the custom for careful housekeepers to burn dried lavender and other aromatic herbs whenever domestic smells became intolerable. (This practice continued, in fact, until the improvement of sanitary arrangements and the discovery of good disinfectants made it no longer necessary.) To make the chore a little easier, eighteenth-century tradesmen prepared small 'pastilles', made of charcoal, benzoin and gum arabic, that could be ignited and then allowed to smoulder away gently, giving off an aromatic smoke that produced the same effect.

For burning these pastilles in, nineteenth-century manufacturers of pottery and porcelain produced many delightful little replicas of cottages and castles, the majority of them in bone china. Each of these had in its interior a shallow recess, in which the pastille would be placed, and usually one or more chimneys or towers through which the smoke could escape. The Victorians delighted in these charming little appliances—those from the Rockingham factory being especially beautiful—and pastille burners (crusted, often, with tiny flowers) were to be found in the majority of homes.

It was the members of the American Forces stationed in Britain during the Second World War who first started to collect nineteenth-century cottage and castle pastille burners with great enthusiasm. Seeing in these decorative little objects admirable souvenirs of their stay in the United Kingdom, the visitors bought every pastille burner on which they could lay their hands. Prices immediately started to soar, and as soon as manufacturing returned more or less to normal after the end of hostilities modern replicas came on to the market in great quantities. No large sum should be paid for any 'Victorian' pastille burner, therefore, unless the purchaser is as certain as he or she can be that it is genuinely 'old'.

CHAPTER EIGHTEEN

LITHOPHANES

These strange 'porcelain pictures' can still be found occasionally, and are often unrecognised for what they really are. If it is examined closely the surface of a lithophane will be seen to vary in thickness according to the intentions of the designer. When the picture is held up to a strong light the parts where the porcelain is very thin will appear light and the parts that are very thick will appear dark. Between these extremes a wide range of 'middle tones' will be produced, and with them some very subtle and dramatic effects may be obtained.

Known sometimes by the alternative name 'Berlin transparencies' (this indicates clearly where they originated), lithophanes were first brought to the notice of the trade in Britain in 1828 when a Robert Griffiths Jones applied for a patent to protect a process for making them. By 1850 they were extremely popular. Most were imported from Germany, but they were produced, too, by a number of British firms, working under licence. Among the lithophane pictures known to have been marketed by Messrs. Minton are those with the endearing titles 'Mother and Dying Child', 'The Agony in the Garden' and 'The Jolly Good Fellow'. Other companies that concerned themselves with the lithophane trade were Copelands, Wedgwoods and Graingers of Worcester, and they were also made at a small factory at Llanelly in South Wales and in Ireland at Belleek.

The larger and more elaborate lithophanic novelties produced by these factories—such as pictorial ceramic lampshades and night-light shades—are rather scarce and tend to be expensive, but the smaller plaques and panels that were made and marketed in much greater quantities are still within the reach of the average collector. If these are displayed in specially designed illuminated cases or are placed where they will be suitably lit they can be relied on to make unusually attractive features even in a contemporary decorative scheme.

CHAPTER NINETEEN

GOSS CHINA

Fortunate, indeed, is the collector who fills a cupboard with perfect examples of some entirely neglected ware or some forgotten manufacturer's products, and then finds very shortly afterwards that public attention has been drawn, quite by chance, to the subjects of his collection, and that the pieces in his chosen field have started to rise rapidly in value. Collectors of 'Goss China' (that made by William Henry Goss and Company, of Stoke-on-Trent) are lucky, in that prices of all but the finest early pieces are still relatively low. But they have risen appreciably lately. And there is no knowing to what levels they may not climb.

Best known of Goss products are the 'china' souvenirs produced for sale to visitors to the principal cities, resorts and watering places. These flowed out from the Goss factory in an unceasing variety of shapes and sizes, novelties such as 'shoes' designed to hold (real) match-boxes being especially popular. The words 'A Present From . . .' are to be found on many of these little mementoes, and on most of them there are brightly coloured armorial bearings. No one could claim convincingly that these Goss gift-trade pieces are outstandingly beautiful. They are not—they are decidedly 'ordinary'. But they bring back the days when a 'trip to the seaside' was a treat to be looked forward to for months, and to be recalled with the greatest pleasure for an equally long time. Their attraction, then, is more nostalgic than aesthetic—but is not that true of so many late Victorian pieces?

On a slightly higher level, the 'jewelled porcelain' produced by Messrs. Goss is now attracting the attention of collectors. At Sèvres, earlier, pieces of porcelain had been decorated with imitation emeralds and rubies, but these 'gems', which were only fixed on with a flux, and then given a certain degree of anchorage by a final firing, were still liable to drop off, or to be knocked off, leaving evident gaps. In Goss's method recesses in which 'jewels' could be set were specially made in the porcelain before it was fired, and his wares have usually remained in their pristine condition.

CHAPTER TWENTY

MOCHA WARE

During the greater part of Queen Victoria's reign many factories in the Staffordshire Potteries were busily engaged in producing enormous quantities of cheap earthenware for export to the neediest parts of what was then known as the 'British Empire'. One of the most effective forms of decoration applied to these mass-produced vessels was carried out with a strong infusion of hops and tobacco. 'Mocha ware'— that is the name usually given to pieces decorated in this rudimentary way—is now properly appreciated by collectors.

When the article was ready to be decorated it would be turned slowly on a lathe. As it rotated, the workman would apply to it a broad band of alkaline 'slip' (that is, clay reduced with water to the consistency of thin cream). Near the edge of this band, he, or she, would apply with a brush a few spots of the hops and tobacco tincture. When the dark brown dye entered the damp slip it would travel rapidly, like the branches of a tree growing outwards, or like the fronds of a fern. No special artistic skill was needed for this, and as only one firing was needed to protect the decoration, the technique was one that particularly commended itself to the manufacturer keen on a quick, profitable turnover.

CHAPTER TWENTY-ONE

DOULTON POTTERY

One of the liveliest potteries in England during the nineteenth century was situated in Lambeth, where Messrs. Doultons were busy producing serviceable pieces intended for the ordinary domestic trade. During the last thirty years of Queen Victoria's reign, however, the directors of the pottery were a little more ambitious. Their plan, during those decades, was to produce individual pieces of greater artistic merit that would appeal to collectors. They declared their new policy like this, in the *Art Journal*:

> 'It is not their intention to produce them in sets or to make duplicates, in order that the unique character of these products may be sustained; having in perspective the time when such wares may be sought for and gathered into collections and museums.'

The firm specialised in producing a high-quality salt-glazed stoneware of great refinement. To create their new, artistic pieces, the directors approached many of the promising young students who were leaving the rapidly developing government-aided schools of art and design. By offering these students secure employment, and by encouraging them to develop their own particular talents, Doultons built up a loyal team of creative designers who made the firm's name famous in many different parts of the world. At the beginning of 1882 there were over two hundred female decorative artists employed in the Doulton potteries.

With the work of so many different designers to choose from, the collector of signed Doulton pieces has an interesting and wide field of study. The work of the more famous Doulton artists—such as the modeller George Tinworth, for example, who took time off from producing plaques and other commissioned works for churches in order to turn out some delightful little groups of comic mice—tends to come on the market rarely, and to fetch very high prices when it does. The work of some of the less well known designers may be equally interesting, but it can still be bought for less, piece for piece, than many of the mass-produced wares of our contemporary potteries. The initials, monograms and signs with which Doulton artists put their personal autographs on their work can be quickly identified by reference to Geoffrey A. Godden's *Encyclopaedia of British Pottery and Porcelain Marks*, published in 1964.

CHAPTER TWENTY-TWO

VICTORIAN TEAPOTS

The Victorian Age was a great time for tea-drinking. Wealthy people waited eagerly for each new season's crop of leaves to arrive. (They were brought, amid great excitement, by the famous sailing clippers such as the *Cutty Sark*, which raced half-way round the world in a desperate attempt to be the first home.) Less wealthy people were able to enjoy at last a beverage that had been for a century and a half one of the most expensive of luxuries. With tea firmly established, then, as one of the most popular national drinks, pots in which it could be brewed were produced in an exciting variety of shapes and sizes. No collection of Victoriana would be complete without a few representative examples.

'BARGE' TEAPOTS

These giant pots—made, usually, to hold either a half gallon or a gallon of tea—were produced in the Black Country, principally near Burton-on-Trent. They are said to derive their name from the people in the gaily painted canal boats who bought so many of them, but messages pressed into specially provided flat panels on their sides show that many of them were commissioned as gifts for house-proud matrons in Balham and Brixton and other rapidly developing suburbs. Most barge teapots are treacle-finished with a rich brown glaze and have crudely fashioned but brightly

A 'barge' teapot.

coloured birds, flowers, butterflies and other decorative features applied in 'spotted dog' fashion over their rotund surfaces. Many barge teapots have, on their lids, knobs that are made as miniature replicas of themselves. There are few contemporary interiors in which a barge teapot will not sit quite happily, and good specimens are changing hands, in consequence, at rapidly ascending prices.

A late Victorian teapot made in the shapes of two characters from Gilbert and Sullivan's opera *Patience*.

CHAPTER TWENTY-THREE

VICTORIAN DOOR FURNITURE

No serious collector of Victoriana should fail to look out for the delightful porcelain finger-plates, door knobs and key-hole covers made, after 1867, at Messrs. Lea Smith and Boulton's Crown Works at Burslem. This firm, later purchased by Messrs. Gaskell, Son and Co., also made and marketed porcelain lamp stands, umbrella knobs and other small goods which have not yet received too much attention.

CHAPTER TWENTY-FOUR

VICTORIAN WORK-TABLES AND THEIR CONTENTS

One of the most welcome presents a young, nineteenth-century bride could receive was a domestic work-table. Made, perhaps, from rosewood or some other very choice

The Victorian lady, advised by Mrs. Beeton that 'light' needle-work—and none other—was appropriate in the drawing-room, would probably use a graceful little pair of scissors, like this, for snipping her wools and silks.

wood, or surfaced with Chinese lacquer, a table of this kind would contain a number of useful and beautifully made implements and accessories. (A typical set of fittings might include a dainty mother-of-pearl needle case, bound with gold; a button-box; one or more egg-shaped thimble-holders

A beautifully embroidered pen-wiper from a Victorian work-box
or work-table.

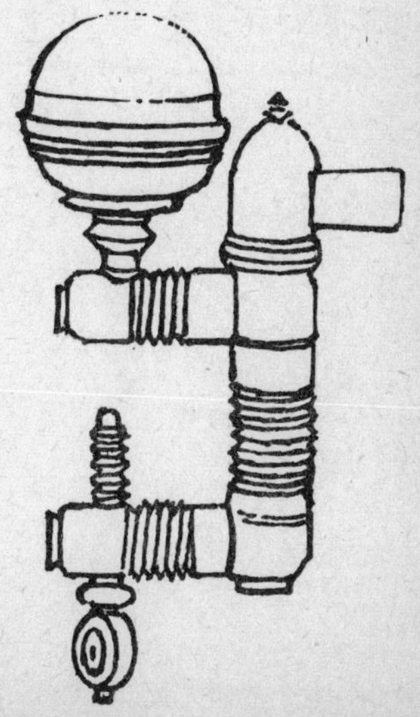

A wooden cramp from an early Victorian work-table.

made, possibly, of ivory or tortoiseshell; a measure; a pin-cushion and a box or two for pins; a pair of scissors with a decorative sheath; a bunch of lace bobbins, weighted, per-haps, with Bristol glass beads; a pen-wiper; and a beautifully made cramp that would be screwed to the edge of a working surface so that it provided a raised, rounded form like a mushroom, to act as a sewing aid.) Not many of these work-tables exist today with their contents intact, but the collector of Victoriana who is prepared to search diligently in junk shops and second-hand goods shops will probably find enough of their scattered pieces to be able to furnish at least one.

CHAPTER TWENTY-FIVE

VICTORIAN JEWELLERY

During the first half of this century Victorian jewellery tended to be less warmly appreciated than it is today. All too often the contents of ladies' 'trinket boxes' were given or thrown away when their owners passed on. 'Those old bits and pieces of Grandmother's,' they might be called, disparagingly. 'Far too fussy,' they were thought, and 'Vulgar' and 'Lacking in taste' were other harsh judgments that were commonly applied to them.

But the Second World War and its immediate aftermath brought a great change in the general outlook. With scarcely any new jewellery or dress ornaments of any kind to be seen in British shops, people were forced to examine more closely any older, unwanted pieces that might still be lying in odd cluttered corners of the home. To the amazement of the fashion writers, the richness of Victorian jewellery that had been previously called 'fussy' and the colourfulness that had been called 'vulgar' were found to be highly desirable qualities in an age of drab austerity. Today the discarded 'bits and pieces' of the pre-war days are seized on with delight, and the market value of the best of them has risen with astonishing rapidity.

This Victorian jewellery shows fewer signs of being affected by the new processes of industrialisation than comparable examples of any other important craft. Every piece that was made with gold and set with precious or semi-precious stones had to be worked, in almost every respect, by hand. The techniques that had been developed by skilled hands over many centuries were so subtle and exact that it

The Victorian jewellery-maker would lavish many hours of loving work on a cameo necklace of this kind.

was not seen, at first, how they could be assimilated into the new and vulgarised world of the machine. The jeweller's standards of design and workmanship did not deteriorate as quickly, therefore, as did most of the other traditional craftsmen who were to be made practically redundant by the Industrial Revolution. By collecting Victorian jewellery we are in touch with an earlier age of individuality and elegance.

The term 'semi-precious', used so often in connection with Victorian jewellery, needs, perhaps, to be defined. It is never applied, in knowledgeable circles, to mass-produced costume or fashion jewellery, set with paste 'gems' or marcasites. It is applied, properly, to all jewellery made with real gemstones other than diamonds, rubies, emeralds and sapphires (which, by their rarity and consequent high value, qualify for the desirable label 'precious').

Semi-precious stones that were especially popular in Victorian times were the amethyst, the garnet, the topaz, the peridot and the tourmaline. The amethyst was the most popular, perhaps, of all. It was the birthstone of those born in the month of February. Cut, usually, with long inclined facets that brought out their delicate purple or lilac shades to perfection, amethysts were especially suitable for the 'rivière' necklaces (necklaces, that is, made of a number of large, similar stones, separately and unobtrusively mounted) that were produced in such great numbers during the last thirty years of Queen Victoria's reign.

CHAPTER TWENTY-SIX

CORAL

During two whole decades in the middle of the nineteenth century jewellery made with coral was extremely fashionable. (It is believed that a wedding present of coral ornaments given by a Prince of the Sicilies to his French bride in 1845 was chiefly responsible for the sudden popularity of this pleasant material.) In spite of the caustic comments of certain writers, who castigated the people who went about 'bedizened with twisted sticks of seeming red sealing-wax', the Age of Coral has been treated sympathetically by the art-historians. If we find a genuine piece of mid-Victorian coral jewellery today we may regard ourselves as particularly fortunate.

In examining one of these early examples of coral jewellery we will probably notice at once that it falls into one of these three clearly defined categories:

(*a*) It will be made from coral in its original or 'branched' form—resembling, usually, pink or reddish twigs. (Natural coral has been carried on the person since classical times, to protect the wearer from danger, or from any possible effects of the 'Evil Eye'.)

(*b*) It will be made from a single piece of coral, polished so that it forms a smooth, useful object, such as a ring on which a child would be able to cut its teeth, or from a number of polished pieces (as, for example, a necklace made of coral beads).

(*c*) It will be made from a piece or pieces of coral carved by a highly skilled workman or workmen so that it resembles a flower, a hand, a crucifix or some other decorative or significant form. Most of the carved Victorian coral pieces we may find will have been produced in Italy (Genoa and Naples were the principal centres), but we may be lucky enough to stumble across an example of the work of Robert Phillips, who had an establishment in Cockspur Street, London. Phillips' carved coral pieces were shown all over Europe, and received many awards.

CHAPTER TWENTY-SEVEN

JET

The word 'jet' is applied nowadays to aircraft without external airscrews that move at extremely fast speeds. One hundred years ago it had—in everyday use—a different meaning. The Victorians were greatly preoccupied with the inevitable approach of death, with the tragic circumstances in which death could take place, and with keeping alive the memory of the dear departed. Jet, to them, was a beautiful, hard, black material that was especially suitable for mourning wear. The widows who, like their Queen, were reluctant to discard their weeds found it almost indispensable as a source of dramatically sombre ornament. (For some years after her husband died the Queen asked that ladies who were to be presented to her should wear no pearls, no rubies, no diamonds—only jet.) A wealthy widow, deprived of the chance to deck herself out with brilliant gems, might adorn herself instead with an enormous quantity of jet brooches, jet bracelets, jet necklaces, jet ear-rings, jet clasps and a miscellaneous assortment of jet crosses and other insignia. All these may turn up today, to add a valuable period flavour to a contemporary jewel-box.

To be as scientifically exact as the average collector of Victoriana will ever need to be, it is sufficient to know that jet is a kind of extremely hard coal. It has been found, principally, in two quite separate parts of the world—in

Galicia (in Spain), and in Whitby, on the sea-coast of Yorkshire. The jet found in Spain has always been appreciably softer and cheaper than that found at Whitby. Whitby jet has normally been used, therefore, for the choicer pieces to be carved or given a fine and lasting polish. Galician jet has been used, in preference, for the necklaces that have been produced by the hundred and thousand.

The earliest jet ornaments made at Whitby can be dated more or less exactly to the first decade of the nineteenth century, when a publican called Carter and an artist by the name of Jefferson collaborated in the production of some experimental pieces that seem, today, quite crudely carved. Primitive these pre-Victorian pieces may have been, but they proved to be eminently saleable, and soon a small factory was set up in Carter's home from which jet articles that showed slightly higher standards of craftsmanship were sent to appreciative customers in many different parts of the country and even—occasionally—abroad.

By the time Prince Albert's Great Exhibition of the Arts and Sciences was attracting large crowds to London's Hyde Park there were at least four dozen factories producing jet jewellery at Whitby. Twenty years later there were nearly four times as many. With jet jewellery on offer in the great majority of the town's shop windows (outdoing even such homely necessities as bread and beef), the little watering place had a distinctly funereal appearance.

Not all the 'jet' articles we may find in second-hand goods shops and street markets today will be, in fact, really jet. Some lovely Victorian pieces were made in black glass. This resembles jet closely, and is usually taken for it. The most careful collectors of Victoriana will, however, refer to the synthetic substitute as 'French' jet.

CHAPTER TWENTY-EIGHT

KEEPSAKES AND MEMENTOES

The Victorian Age was one of the most sentimental and emotional that the human race has known. No drawing-room entertainment of that era was considered to be complete unless it had its proper quota of tear-jerking songs. No domestic interior was thought to be fully furnished without a number of harrowing pictures—of stags at bay, possibly, or of dogs mourning over the bodies of their lately deceased masters.

This preoccupation with the romantic and anecdotal even affected the design of Victorian jewellery. During the early decades of the great Queen's reign the hair of a beloved person was regarded as something too precious to be lightly thrown away, and countless brooches, bracelets and other ornaments were made from the shorn locks of sweethearts, relatives who had gone abroad or dear departed friends. Later in the reign it became fashionable to wear gold brooches and lockets in which hair could also be preserved, but more reticently. It is still possible to find occasionally one of the charming Victorian keepsakes in which one or more miniature portraits are set in delicate frames given an additional richness with pearls and precious or semi-precious stones.

The richer Victorians were great travellers, and they brought back from their holidays in Europe a great number of pieces of ornamental jewellery made specially to act as souvenirs of the resorts they had visited. From Switzerland they would bring back ivory 'edelweiss' and other flowers carved by the skilful craftsmen of that country; from Italy, brooches and bracelets that incorporated charming little mosaics; from Pompeii, pieces of 'jewellery' that featured lava instead of gems; if they went farther afield they would come back with even more unusual or exotic mementoes with which to deck themselves. Quite a large proportion of Victorian personal jewellery is influenced by North African and Assyrian styles. The discoveries made during the excavation of Nineveh proved to be particularly exciting. It would be difficult to count the number of different types of lotus flower that bloomed on fashionable Victorian bosoms.

CHAPTER TWENTY-NINE

PINCHBECK

The word 'pinchbeck' has been used so often recently to mean 'sham' or 'false' that it has lost a little of its lustre. Used correctly, it is applied to all articles made of the special alloy of copper and zinc discovered by the London watchmaker, Christopher Pinchbeck, early in the eighteenth century. Pinchbeck's alloy closely resembles gold, and does not tarnish readily, as do other 'imitations' of the precious metal. Many charming brooches, bracelets, and other small articles were made in pinchbeck during the Victorian era. Most have survived, because their intrinsic value has never been high enough to warrant their being melted down for recovery purposes.

CHAPTER THIRTY

JAPANNED WARE

During the seventeenth and eighteenth centuries lacquered goods brought to Britain from China, Japan and other parts of the Far East by the British East India Company attracted much interest and admiration. Many attempts were made to imitate the exquisite surface texture of these lovely pieces. Wooden chests and cabinets were given innumerable smooth coats of black varnish paint; papier mâché trays and tables were similarly 'japanned'; it was not until William Allgood perfected his method of applying an extremely hard, heat-resistant varnish to a surface of tinned iron that 'japanned ware' (as we understand the term today) became one of the country's more important subjects of trade, exported by the crateful to all parts of the civilised world.

No one who buys a single genuine piece of nineteenth-century japanned ware for a collection of Victoriana should be allowed to remain unaware of the inhumane circumstances in which it may have been produced.

First, the article would be made from thinly rolled iron sheet, plated with tin, joints in early work being usually carried out by the comparatively simple process of folding and riveting, later work being usually neatly trimmed and brazed.

Then the metal would be given as many as fifteen separate coats of varnish. After each coat was applied the article would be placed in an oven in the middle of a blazing charcoal furnace and it would be left there, while the varnish was thoroughly baked, for as long as a month. Between each baking, and the subsequent application of another coat of varnish the hardened surfaces would be rubbed down carefully by women and children, using only their hands as polishing pads, and using cold water only (and it was extremely cold, too, in winter time) as a lubricant. The poor people employed to do this uncomfortable work tended to sicken and die at an early age as a result of the cumulative poisons they absorbed into their systems, but the lustrous, translucent surfaces they produced by their ill-rewarded labours would, for sheer loveliness, be difficult to surpass.

Once the Allgood process had been perfected, japanned goods in a number of delightful ground colours were produced at Pontypool in South Wales, the nearby town of Usk, Birmingham, Wolverhampton and other centres. The decorations applied to the best japanned work are invariably delightful. A japanned vase or coffee-pot, with a rich black ground relieved with sprays of gold, silver or coloured flowers and butterflies, may well be the most admired piece in any privately acquired collection of nineteenth-century household ware.

The more important examples of Pontypool and Usk japanned ware—kettles and canisters, coffee urns, brazier sets and comparable pieces—are likely to be too expensive (when they come on the market) to be of much interest to the collector of average means. They may not even qualify as 'Victoriana', anyway—the South Wales japanned ware industry was at its busiest before the Queen's reign, and cannot therefore be solely associated with that distinctive period of history. The japanned tin trays produced in enormous quantities in the Midlands during the 1820s, 1830s and 1840s may be found much more easily, and bought for prices well within the pocket-money range. Among the most notable examples to look for are:

> The 'Willow Pattern' trays produced for Messrs. Jennens and Bettridge of Birmingham.
> The trays decorated with coaching scenes by Robert Noys.
> The transfer-printed trays produced after 1834 at Bilston in Staffordshire. (The trays that showed a Bengal tiger in the act of seizing its prey were exported by the hundred to all parts of what was then the British Empire.)

Japanned ware goods, like so many others classified loosely today as 'Victoriana', may be easily passed over, with their special qualities unrecognised, by those who have not taken the trouble to make a special study of this particular aspect of industrial history. To those who have, they are an unending source of delight.

CHAPTER THIRTY-ONE

TUNBRIDGE WARE

Occasionally a collector searching for Victoriana will find some small useful or ornamental article, such as a workbox, a tray, a tea caddy or a candlestick, that has been decorated with a fine mosaic made of pieces of wood of various tones and colours. Probably this will have originated at or near the town of Tunbridge, in Kent, during the Victorian period, the district then being renowned for this distinctive ware.

The production of 'English mosaic'—as Tunbridge Ware was sometimes called—involved the gathering of a great variety of woods. (At one time, it is said, no fewer than 160 kinds were available to the veneer-maker.) These woods would first be cut into thin strips. Then the craftsman—or 'bandmaker', as he was often called—would glue a number of the strips together, using a pattern drawn on squared paper to ensure that he was arranging them correctly. Then he would slice the block across vertically, at regular intervals, and, later, when he had rearranged and reglued the slices, he would saw the block cross-wise into very thin sheets, each cut producing an identically patterned veneer. (If you find this hard to understand, imagine yourself taking a few paper-thin slices off the end of a stick of Blackpool rock!) The wooden articles surfaced with these veneers are among the most attractive—to present-day eyes—of any produced during the mid-Victorian era.

CHAPTER THIRTY-TWO

COVENTRY RIBBONS

When the Edict of Nantes was revoked in 1685 many skilled Huguenot silk-weavers fled from France to Britain, bringing with them advanced techniques that were to be brought to an unprecedented degree of perfection just two centuries later by an enterprising Coventry manufacturer called Thomas Stevens. Today the admirable series of decorative and intricately detailed 'picture ribbons' that bear Stevens' name can be guaranteed to cause a lot of excitement and to fetch very high prices when they appear in the salerooms. (Thousands were marketed by Stevens for only sixpence or a shilling each in the years after the Great Exhibition of 1851.)

Collectors of Stevengraphs have a very wide range of subjects to search for—a recent sale included portraits of members of the Royal Family and other notable people; hunting and coaching scenes; pictures of football, cricket and other popular sports; and studies of well-known railway engines. The vivid hues and tints of the silks used in the Stevens factory have held up well to the passage of time: in many instances these most attractive pictures look almost as fresh and colourful as they did when they first left the Coventry looms. Technically speaking, the Victorian era was a remarkable age!

CHAPTER THIRTY-THREE

SAMPLERS

The name 'sampler' was given, in the first place, to a piece of embroidery in which a number of different stitches and designs had been worked, and which was intended to act as a source of reference for work to be carried out in the future (the word is actually derived from the Latin noun *exemplum*, which means something meant to serve as a pattern or example). Long before printed pattern books were known, young ladies learning needlework were encouraged to produce these samplers, as copying existing forms of embroidery was the only known method of acquiring a knowledge of traditional techniques. During the early years of Queen Victoria's reign many splendid samplers were carried out in nurseries, in schools and in sewing rooms. Where these have been carefully preserved, they can be used as attractive centres of interest in any present-day decorative scheme.

Examined closely, one of these nineteenth-century samplers may well be found to have been carried out almost entirely in 'cross stitch'—a stitch (with tent stitch) associated so consistently with latter-day samplers that it is sometimes referred to as 'sampler stitch'. The fascinating variety of stitches found in earlier samplers had virtually disappeared. (Stem and chain stitches would be used to outline leaves and flowers in eighteenth-century samplers, for example, and French knots might be used for picking out details. In work carried out in the second half of the nineteenth century all these niceties are rarely found.) The reason for this uniformity of surface is easy to understand. Samplers were no longer needed as sources of reference. They were intended, instead, principally for display. They might even be carried out on specially prepared canvas or linen, on which 'guide lines' had been previously printed, and in this case they would probably be worked according to detailed instructions provided in a carefully compiled booklet.

The new approach to sampler-making encouraged the young embroiderer to be pictorially inventive, rather than technically proficient. Normally a Victorian sampler will be framed with a conventional border pattern on all four sides (formalised 'carnation' and 'strawberry' patterns were universally popular), and inside this frame there will be a number of conventionally drawn animals, birds, trees, pots of flowers with, perhaps, a simplified representation of the sewer's home. Inside the frame, too, there will be (again, almost invariably) some motto, biographical or autobiographical note or pious sentiment that makes the sampler different from any that has ever been produced before, anywhere, and unlike any sampler that is being cherished now by any other collector.

There are, for instance, some delightful Victorian samplers produced by very young embroiderers. The words patiently stitched on these are very often charming:

> *The trees were green,*
> *The sun was hot,*
> *Sometimes I worked,*
> *And sometimes not.*

Sometimes a young person's sampler will very obviously have been produced under the eagle eye of a vigilant adult:

Collectors today are usually pleased when they find samplers worked with messages that reflect the Victorians' preoccupation with the closeness of death:

The morbid nature of such messages—dealing, often, with the darkness of the tomb, the covering power of the shroud or the appetite of the worm—usually makes an odd contrast with the gay and decorative flowers, birds and shells that are worked round the words and between the verses. But that contrast is typical of the age. (One Victorian sampler asks plaintively: 'The grass is green, the rose is red, Where is my work when I am dead?')

Richly worked Victorian samplers in contemporary frames tend to be expensive. Unframed samplers may not be priced as highly, but they are likely not to have remained so clean. The tendency of wool to collect dirt was worrying sampler-makers even before the end of the nineteenth century. In the *Dictionary of Needlework* compiled by Caulfield and Saward in 1882 we find that embroiderers are recommended to treat any of their wool work that may have become badly soiled thus:

> 'Wash it with gin and soft soap, in the proportion of one quarter of a pound of soft soap to half a pint of gin.'

What, this makes one wonder, would such a cleansing technique cost anyone rash enough to use it today?

CHAPTER THIRTY-FOUR

PATCHWORK

Women and girls, one hundred years ago, were not generally accustomed to going out to work (except, possibly, into 'domestic service' or nursing), as so many are today. There was more time, then, for producing 'patchwork'—a name that covers a wide variety of sewn household goods, made almost invariably in the home or in the school.

The principal source of supply for patchwork pieces has always been the scraps and oddments of material that have been left over after dressmaking, curtain-hanging and furniture-covering have been completed. (Some patchwork enthusiasts have been known to buy small pieces of material when these have been needed to complete a pattern, but it would clearly be incorrect to go shopping for all the materials, a procedure that would have drawn this scornful reproach from George Eliot's Maggie Tulliver: 'It's foolish work . . . tearing things to pieces to sew 'em together again.')

Patchwork reached the Golden Age at the end of the eighteenth century, and in the early years of the nineteenth century, but it could hardly be said to be in a state of decline during the period with which we are immediately concerned. The Victorians, sentimental to a fault, saw in patchwork the chance to use, preserve and wax tearful over materials that had long been familiar and should, properly, have been thrown away and forgotten, or had some special family significance. (A hexagonal piece of silk, brocade or velvet in a patchwork quilt might be marked—for instance—'From Father's Wedding Vest' or 'From my very first Party Dress'. Any piece of Victorian patchwork that has survived to the present time in a reasonable condition is worthy of the most careful preservation. It is almost certain to be a significant human document, as well as an example of handiwork of some intrinsic beauty.)

At the beginning of Queen Victoria's reign, then, ladies who had the time were liable to spend a great part of their days doing patchwork. A Miss Hutton, who died in 1846 at the age of ninety, wrote a detailed description of the work she had done with her needle, saying that she had 'made patchwork beyond calculation'. In many homes at that time, the children were put to work immediately they returned from their lessons. ('As soon as the lamp was lighted, out came the patchwork.') One lady who died at the age of eighty early in the 1900s is believed to have finished one patchwork quilt for every year of her life.

The words 'patchwork' and 'quilt' are linked together so consistently that one might be forgiven for thinking that there were no other forms of patchwork to be found and collected. Of course, this just is not true. Besides quilts, there are patchwork curtains, bed-hangings, chair covers and piano-stool covers, antimacassars, cushion covers, wall hangings, shawls, waistcoats, pincushions, bags of all kinds and bell-pulls. The excellent book nominated in the 'Suggestions For Further Reading' on page 127 contains a large number of splendid pictures of different pieces of patchwork carried out in a wide variety of techniques.

CHAPTER THIRTY-FIVE

BERLIN WOOL-WORK

During the first twenty years of Queen Victoria's reign Berlin wool-work was all the rage. (It had become so popular by 1847 that a lady writing a preface to an *Illuminated Book of Needlework* was able to begin: 'Embroidery, or as it is more often called Berlin wool work, has been brought to such a high state of perfection ... the variety of patterns so great, and so well adapted to every purpose to which it can be applied ... that we do not hope here to be able to throw much new light on the subject.')

No serious collector of Victoriana, then, will be able to pursue his or her hobby for long without coming across innumerable examples of this colourful form of needlework. So, it may be useful to know how the craze for Berlin wool-work developed.

The first Berlin patterns were brought into England as early as 1805. They received only a comparatively cool welcome, however, and it was not until 1831, when Mr. Wilks of London's Regent Street started to import directly from Berlin both the patterns and the materials for working them, that the trade really began to thrive. Ten years later more than twelve thousand different designs had been prepared and brought over for sale in the English market.

At that time the patterns were carried out on squared paper not unlike that used in schools today for the drawing of graphs. Each design would be washed in with colour by hand, each square of the pattern being reproduced, eventually, by a single stitch. (Cross stitch and tent stitch were generally used, most of the wools needed for carrying out the designs being made up at Gotha and dyed in Berlin, the rest being prepared in this country.)

Collectors, today, prize the ambitious pictorial designs that were worked in wool and framed for mural display, or for use as fire screens. Some of these 'Berlin work pictures' illustrated historical or Biblical subjects, others had a crudely sentimental appeal. Flowers (in wreaths and bouquets) were especially popular subjects, and gaily coloured birds were used, too, in numerous designs intended to embellish cushions, head rests, foot stools and other small domestic articles. In the Berlin wool-work carried out in the early years of Queen Victoria's reign the backgrounds were usually white or some light tint. In the 1850s and 1860s black backgrounds were consistently preferred, since the contrast between the brilliant colours used in the central motif and its dark surround could be relied on to produce a most dramatic effect. Unfortunately, many of the dyes used to colour the wools for Berlin work have proved to be fugitive, and to find an important example in which the colours retain their original intensity, or anything like it, is something of a triumph.

Occasionally, if you become interested in collecting Victorian needlework, you may come across an example of 'German embroidery'. This name was given to needlework in which beads, strands of silk and other non-woollen materials were incorporated with the Berlin wools to produce a more variegated effect. 'Raised work', too, is sometimes found. In this, some part or parts of the design would be carried out in loose loops. Before the work was completed, these loops would be cut, producing the same effect as a carpet with a particularly deep pile.

Immensely popular as Berlin wool-work was, it evoked a steadily increasing amount of criticism in the latter part of Queen Victoria's reign. 'Is there any real beauty in this, any originality?' queried a dignitary of the Church of England, in a lecture he gave on *Church Work for Ladies*. 'It is simply copy, copy, stitch by stitch. Fancy work without the slightest opportunity to exercise the fancy. Dull task work unenlightened by one spark of freedom and grace.' His strictures were echoed, eventually, all over the country, and forms of embroidery that allowed more scope for originality soon took the place of the ubiquitous 'dull task work'. Today, however, we tend to notice the charms of Berlin wool-work, ignoring the unenterprising attitudes of the ladies who produced it.

CHAPTER THIRTY-SIX

BEADWORK

Beadwork has a long history—some of the finest examples in the Victoria and Albert and other museums date from the Stuart period—but Victorian beadwork, of less historic interest, can still be found in unexpected places and purchased for inconsiderable sums. (The author visited an old lady in North Wales recently and found that her small sitting-room contained a Victorian beadwork firescreen, a Victorian beadwork tea cosy, a Victorian beadwork table centre and several decorative but uncomfortable Victorian beadwork cushions—all inherited from various senior members of her family.)

A favourite dress accessory of the Victorian period was the stocking purse, or 'miser purse'. A purse of this kind was formed like a sausage skin with a small slit in the side through which the coins could be inserted. Invariably, it would be ringed with two movable bands which were used for pushing the coins towards the ends of the purse and for keeping them there. The closed ends of these purses were usually decorated with beadwork fringes or tassels. They are of great interest, because they are quite unlike anything used for carrying money today!

CHAPTER THIRTY-SEVEN

VICTORIAN PICTURES

Not so long ago, Victorian pictures by artists of small repute were thought barely worth looking at. (Paintings and drawings by the leaders of the Pre-Raphaelite Brotherhood and by such well-known masters as Frith and Whistler have never ceased to be quietly appreciated, of course.) Today, after a hectic half century in which Cubists, Futurists, Vorticists and Modernists of many other kinds have brought their startlingly novel works in quick succession before the astonished gaze of a bewildered public, the technical accomplishments and the easily understood naturalism of the minor late-nineteenth-century artists are arousing ever-increasing admiration. Landscapes, flower paintings, still lifes and studies of animals that might have been thrown on the rubbish heap in the years between the wars are now fetching high prices in the salerooms and are being most profitably exported.

Victorian art is so diverse that it would be quite impossible, in a book of this length, to include a catalogue of the various types that have recently attracted the attention of collectors. Here are just a few of the relatively neglected categories of picture that are worth looking out for:

Drawings. Often overlooked because they lack the attractions of colour, Victorian drawings should not be lightly dismissed. Working under the influence, largely, of John

Ruskin, many Victorian artists made pencil, pen and silver-point studies from nature with great intensity and skill.

Engravings of all kinds were produced and sold in large numbers throughout the nineteenth century. Large mezzotints (made, often, to reproduce some admired or popular painting) may still be picked up for a shilling or two, and offer extraordinary value. (The author found recently in a small country saleroom a fine, framed artist's proof signed by William Holman Hunt. It was tied up in a bundle with half a dozen other pictures—most of them photographs of long-forgotten football teams. The lot had failed to attract a single bid.)

Wood Engravings are prints taken (normally) from box-wood blocks. With sharp tools used with an easy movement of the hand, a skilled engraver can produce a wide variety of beautiful surface textures. The greatest wood engraver of all—Thomas Bewick, of Newcastle—had ceased to work before Queen Victoria's reign began, but illustrations cut by the brothers Edward and Thomas Dalziel, John Swain, W. J. Linton and other artists who were influenced by Bewick can still be picked up for a few pence from unsorted collections in unfashionable bric-à-brac shops, while others can be found in second-hand bookstalls, in the volumes in which they were originally published.

Etching, like line engraving, is usually carried out with a copper plate, the ink-retaining channels in this case being bitten into the surface of the plate with a dilute solution of nitric acid. Several prominent artists produced and sold sets of etchings during Queen Victoria's reign, the most famous of all—James McNeill Whistler—producing some superb effects of distance in his remarkable 'Thames Set'.

Lithography, a form of printing in which (during the

nineteenth century) a flat stone was used, was invented by Alois Senefelder at the end of the eighteenth century. During Queen Victoria's reign lithographs of startling virtuosity were being produced in France by Henri Daumier, who worked for the satirical publication called *La Charivari*, and, a little later, by the brilliant observer of the demi-monde, Henri de Toulouse-Lautrec. No lithographs produced in Britain during the Victorian period can rival the work of these outstanding artists, but (largely under the influence of Whistler) a number of sincere and competent British artists did explore the possibilities of this method of picture-making, uniting their efforts eventually in an organisation that they called 'The Senefelder Club'.

CHAPTER THIRTY-EIGHT

SILHOUETTES

The 'silhouette' or profile portrait (carried out, usually, in flat black and contrasted with a light-coloured background) is not a specially Victorian object. In fact, many collectors consider that by the beginning of Victoria's reign the craft of profile-making had passed its best and was already entering its period of decline. But silhouettes were still being produced by the thousand during the early years of the period we are studying, and the best Victorian specimens are not much less attractive than those cut by the better-known professionals fifty and sixty years before. They can still be picked up fairly cheaply, too, and if elegantly framed may make charming decorative features even in a present-day setting. (Please note—no silhouette should be removed from a sound contemporary frame and given a modern replacement. This may well seriously reduce its value.)

The name 'silhouette' was derived originally from the name of Etienne de Silhouette, who became the French Minister of Finance in 1759. De Silhouette's penny-pinching policies proved both unpopular and disastrous, and the public derisively borrowed his name and applied it to the flimsy, paper-thin likenesses that happened, at that time, to be rapidly becoming the rage.

It is not easy for us, today, to appreciate the circumstances in which silhouette-making became, in effect, an international industry—we are so used, now, to cameras and photography that it is difficult to imagine a time when all likenesses had to be taken 'by hand'. Painted portraits of all kinds tended, then, to be expensive—only a very well-to-do couple in the early nineteenth century could afford to employ a professional artist to record in oil colours, on canvas or in pastels the features of their numerous progeny. The best touring silhouette-makers, on the other hand, provided accurate records of their sitters' features and accoutrements for extremely reasonable fees. (As early as 1775, a Mrs. Sarah Harrington was travelling round the country making cut-out portraits that she advertised as 'the most striking likenesses at 2*s*. 6*d*. each'. Augustus Edouart, who cut approximately a quarter of a million silhouette portraits between the years 1825 and 1860, charged, usually, two shillings for a profile bust, and five shillings or more for a full-length study with (perhaps) a small extra fee for the inclusion of a favourite horse or domestic pet. We know exactly what most of the principal figures at the Edinburgh body-snatchers' trial looked like, from the brilliant silhouettes Edouart cut of them during the day-long ordeal.

Sitting, to have a portrait made of oneself, can be a frustrating and exhausting experience. The earliest silhouettes were either cut with almost incredible dexterity using sharp knives or scissors from paper or vellum, or were painted, usually with an intensely black Indian ink or infusion of soot, on a background of white card, vellum, ivory or plaster. These took some little time to execute, during which the sitter had to remain quite motionless. The accuracy, or otherwise, of the silhouette depended entirely on the skill of the cutter or painter.

Later silhouettes were produced with the aid of various mechanical contrivances. To take a fairly typical example, a 'silhouette machine' might depend on a bright light that cast an undistorted shadow of the sitter on a screen. The shape of this shadow could, then, be 'fixed' by a handy operator, or his or her assistant, in a very few seconds. A further mechanical device would then be used to reduce this outline to a more desirable size. Some of the smallest, exquisitely detailed portraits produced in this way are barely any larger than thumb nails. They are well worth collecting. We may not even know the identities of the sitters, but they bring back a vanished bit of history each time we look at them.

Silhouette-making fell out of favour when Monsieur Daguerre, the 'apothecary picture-man', developed his process by which family groups could be recorded pictorially, in not many more seconds, in the full revealing glare of light and shade. After this, the camera took over the job that had been previously performed by the 'black shade maker'. By the end of Queen Victoria's reign the silhouette was a thing of the past.

CHAPTER THIRTY-NINE

BAXTER PRINTS

These are pictures carried out by a special process invented and patented by George Baxter (1804–67). They were at one time much sought after by connoisseurs, and are still worth hunting for today, since the subjects of the pictures included attractive landscapes depicted in great detail, Royal portraits, studies of the Great Exhibition of 1851 and of various Hindoo and Mohammedan buildings, and sentimental scenes from the lives of the poor, taken chiefly from the works of successful contemporary painters. Martyrdoms, too, and the deaths of missionaries are to be found in gory detail in several Baxter prints.

Baxter was the son of a printer who employed skilled craftsmen to colour by hand the pictures he was preparing for publication. The younger man, however, decided to try to find a more economical way of colouring prints, and by 1835 he had developed his new mechanical system. The process, though seeming to save hand labour, did in fact prove very laborious. First, Baxter would print a 'light and shade' version of the picture, using an engraved metal plate charged with brown, blue-grey or some other dark neutral colour. Then he would print more positive colours over this, using one engraved wood block for each hue, shade or tint (sometimes he would use as many as twenty different blocks to print a single picture). The oil-based inks he used produced some particularly rich effects, so that a genuine Baxter print can sometimes be mistaken for an oil-painting if it is not looked at closely.

Baxter was invited to show his prints at the Great Exhibition of 1851 and was awarded a prize. In spite of this success, and the superb prints he produced and marketed in the following year, his business gradually failed and the patents passed out of his hands.

CHAPTER FORTY

SAND PICTURES

The Victorians had one particularly strange kink about pictures. As so many pictures had been produced in previous centuries with oil-paints, water-colours, pastels and other conventional media, they tended to admire any picture that might be produced in their own times with some entirely novel material. Sand pictures were known as early as the reign of George III, when they were used in the elaborate table decorations produced for the dining-rooms of the wealthy. In Victorian times they became popular with all classes who could afford them, but they are particularly associated with certain seaside resorts.

When a sand picture was being planned the outlines would be drawn first with a pencil or pen on a piece of stiff paper or card. Next, adhesive paste or glue would be spread over all the surfaces to be 'coloured', and before this had had a chance to dry different kinds of sand would be sprinkled on to it, each part of the picture being covered with sand of a tone or texture that seemed to the artist to be particularly suitable. Alum Bay, in the Isle of Wight, was an important centre for the supply of these sands, which might range from an almost pure white to a dark tone that was very nearly black.

Sand pictures were produced in a wide variety of subjects, simple landscapes and sentimentalised animals being particularly popular. Those still in their original frames are becoming scarcer, as many have been collected recently for export to America.

CHAPTER FORTY-ONE

THEATRICAL PLAYBILLS AND POSTERS

There was not much subtlety about the melodramas that Victorian audiences crowded to see—in *East Lynne* and the other popular tragedies that are revived, even today, with wholly irreverent bravura, right was right and wrong was wrong, and there was no thought of any of our modern 'nonsense' about compassion for the evil-doer. The bills put up to announce these theatrical offerings were as bold and as uncomprising as the entertainments they were intended to advertise. (Often, one of these bills would contain a crude picture of a murder, betrayal or some other exciting incident.) They are so much admired today that they are being reproduced in great quantities by modern methods, the replicas being sold to be used as wall decorations and, even, as kitchen cloths.

One of the principal differences between Victorian theatrical entertainments and those of the present day is made immediately noticeable by these old playbills and by their modern replicas—the programmes, in those far-off and more leisurely days, were considerably longer. No one went to the Victorian theatre to see only one play, as we do today! From the author's collection—to take a single example—a bill issued for the THEATRE ROYAL, DRURY LANE announces for THIS EVENING:

Sir Peter Teazle, Mr. W. Farren:
Charles Surface, Mr. C. Kemble; etc., etc. . . .

After which, POPPING THE QUESTION.

· To conclude with, THE FORTY THIEVES.

Miss Betts, announcing her BENEFIT (the first she had taken) at the THEATRE ROYAL ENGLISH OPERA-HOUSE, had the honour to promise her Friends and Public a favourite Opera. After which, a MUSICAL MELANGE. To conclude with a MUSICAL AFTERPIECE. Tickets and private boxes were to be had of Miss Betts herself, at 20 Norfolk Street, Strand.

One wonders how many the good lady sold.

CHAPTER FORTY-TWO

VICTORIAN DOLLS AND TOYS

The nursery was one of the most important features of the normal Victorian home (anyone with a family who could possibly afford to do so would set aside one room, at least, in which the children could be kept, during the greatest part of each day, in closely guarded isolation). Any nursery that contained one or more girls would inevitably contain a number of dolls. Many of these have survived, and are highly valued today by adult collectors. With their numerous layers of petticoats, made of longcloth, flannel and cambric, ornamented with feather-stitching and hand-embroidery, they can hardly be called under-dressed. Wax dolls, with their delicately modelled features, are especially attractive, and so are the delightful little perambulators and carriages in which they were wheeled by their proud young owners (though genuine Victorian examples of these are now rare, and expensive).

The first doll that could say 'Papa' and 'Mama' attracted a lot of attention at an Industrial Exhibition in Paris shortly before Queen Victoria's accession. To work the mechanism one had to lift the arms of the doll, the right arm operating a kind of internal bellows to produce the sound of one word, the left arm producing by a similar process the sound of the other. After similar dolls had been seen in Great Britain the manufacture of ingenious mechanical toys played an important part in the thriving nursery trade.

Other toys popular in Victorian nurseries that are definitely worth looking out for, and preserving, are sets of childrens' blocks and bricks; solitaire boards; the little wooden model trains that were designed to be pulled across floors on the ends of pieces of string; Noah's Arks, with their intriguing complements of carved wooden animals; the wooden or ivory shapes used for the game of spillikins; and tops and skipping ropes of various kinds. A real Victorian rocking horse, in good condition, is likely to be as attractive, to present-day eyes, as any of the more laboured pieces of academic sculpture that were prepared specially for the great international exhibitions.

CHAPTER FORTY-THREE

DOLLS' HOUSES

The dolls' house is believed to have been developed from the 'baby houses' commissioned by, or supplied to, some of the wealthier English families during the eighteenth century. We know that the little princess who was later to become Queen Victoria spent many happy hours playing with her cherished pieces of 'dolls' furniture' at Kensington Palace. By the time her own children were out of their nursery, dolls' houses were to be found in most homes where the royal example was loyally followed. Not many of these nineteenth-century dolls' houses have survived intact—even the best-behaved children tend to be hard on their playthings—and the most splendid examples have passed inevitably into the safe keeping of the authorities of the Victoria and Albert Museum or some other publicly sponsored guardians. Occasionally, though, a genuine piece of Victorian dolls' house furniture may be encountered, or even a whole set. The task of providing a suitable setting for these, if the original dolls' house has disappeared, need not be too difficult—a box, placed on its side, can be lined with some of the excellent miniature wallpapers and ceiling papers produced and marketed by Messrs. Sanderson and Company, and a piece of thin plain felt can be used to cover the 'floor'.

The finest miniature domestic utensils were probably those made for the exquisitely detailed 'kitchens' made at

Nuremberg during the seventeenth and eighteenth centuries. Several British manufacturers were producing miniature pots and pans and tea and dinner services for the toyshop trade during the nineteenth century. These are sometimes confused with the small-scale 'samples' produced for the traveller in more precious goods which may now prove to be valuable collectors' pieces.

CHAPTER FORTY-FOUR

CARD CASES

A most interesting account of the day-to-day life of the Victorian lady is given in Mrs. Isabella Beeton's *Book of Household Management*:

'After luncheon, morning calls and visits may be made and received. These may be divided under three heads: those of ceremony, friendship, and congratulation or condolence. Visits of ceremony or courtesy . . . are uniformly required after dining at a friend's house, or after a ball, picnic, or any other party . . . In all visits, if your acquaintance or friend be not at home, a card should be left. If in a carriage, the servant will answer your inquiry and receive your card: if paying your visits on foot, give your card to the servant in the hall, but leave to go in and rest should on no account be asked . . .'

Calls of the varying kinds required a variety of cards. Here are only a few of Mrs. Beeton's careful instructions on the subject:

'The fashion of visiting cards varies much. They are made extremely thin and highly glazed; but by some enamelled cards are preferred to plain. When calling to enquire at a house during illness, it is usual to turn up the lower right-hand corner of the card, for this denotes that a personal enquiry has been made. Some cards have the words, *Visite, Félicitation, Affaires, Adieu,* printed upon the reverse side, on the corners, so that whichever corner is turned up one of these words appears, and explains the cause of the visit . . .'

To keep her visiting cards clean and uncreased during her frequent and protracted journeys of politeness, the Victorian lady needed a specially designed case—not too bulky or heavy, for this would inconvenience her, but strong, rigid and (above all else) elegant. Card cases were produced, then, in many different materials—gold, ivory and rare woods were prefered by those who could afford them; papier mâché set with mother-of-pearl made an acceptable substitute for those who aspired to the habits of the rich without necessarily having their means. No general collection of Victoriana will be complete without a selection of these graceful little cases, for they played such an important part in the social life of the times.

CHAPTER FORTY-FIVE

SONG COVERS

One of the favourite domestic amusements during the latter half of the nineteenth century was the 'musical evening'. Members of the family would gather round the piano, with or without their friends, to hear each other play and sing the comic songs and sentimental ballads that were the 'Tops of the Pops' of the time.

Among the most prized items in the author's collection of Victoriana is a copy, dated 1852, of Fisher's *Drawing Room Scrap-Book*, an illustrated miscellany of songs and poems which was published annually. One lengthy contribution to this album took the form of a satirical lament called 'The Musical Soirée', which shows that even at the time there were a few percipient souls who found attendance at one of these vocal gatherings painful:

Long dinners, when follow'd by yet longer speeches,
Are tedious enough when you've eaten your fill—
And so are your balls, where the hostess beseeches
You'll not miss one polka or single quadrille.
But what's each of these, or e'en both put together,
Compared to a musical soirée, I ask,
When a bevy of misses, in very hot weather,
Your applause and attention exact as a task? . . .

Critics as unfavourable as that were few, however, and songs and ballads suitable for the 'bevies of misses' poured from the presses as liberally as 'pop' music records do today. Most of these Victorian songs and ballads were marketed in decorative covers and are eagerly sought, today, by collectors. Many of them bore portraits of the theatrical artistes whose renderings had first made the numbers widely known; some were decorated with pictures inspired by the subject matter within. Patriotic songs sung during the time of the Crimean War and the Indian Mutiny showed, usually, on their covers, soldiers and sailors in the picturesque uniforms of the period and are particularly favoured.

CHAPTER FORTY-SIX

DAGUERREOTYPES AND OTHER
EARLY PHOTOGRAPHS

The beginning of Queen Victoria's reign coincided approximately with the first successful demonstrations of what we now call 'photography'. Before the young Queen had had time to be suitably provided with a husband, the Frenchman L. J. M. Daguerre, working in conjunction with J. N. Niepce, had shown that he could preserve a visual image by exposing, in a simple 'camera', a polished silvered copper plate that had been successively iodised and then resensitised with bromide. In England, at about the same time, the inventor Fox Talbot was experimenting successfully with sensitised paper, the name 'calotype' being usually given to early photographs of this type.

It was not until quite late in Queen Victoria's reign that the introduction of more sophisticated processes made it possible for amateurs to take up photography as an interesting hobby. During the intervening decades a visit to the photographers' was a notable occasion—as exacting, almost, as a visit to a portrait painter's or a silhouette-cutter's, since all sitters (or standers) had to keep quite still for several minutes (a close study of a Victorian 'family group' will often reveal the metal supports used to collar wavering necks or to hold fidgeting feet and hands in required positions).

Today many admirable collections are being made of these early photographs. The care that had to be taken in the arrangement of their subjects, and in providing suitable lighting, has ensured that those that have survived are treated as considerable works of art. They provide an incomparable record of the dress and manners of the whole period, too. For the keen collector of Victoriana, they are an invaluable source of information.

CHAPTER FORTY-SEVEN

VINAIGRETTES

There is a famous painting that shows Cardinal Wolsey walking near a number of Londoners. No doubt, at that time his walk among the inhabitants of the great Tudor city would have reminded him unpleasantly of the plagues that, from time to time, drastically reduced its population. Almost certainly, the people would not smell as sweetly as a similar crowd would smell today, for they would wash only on comparatively rare occasions—if, in fact, they washed at all. To protect himself from the general unsavouriness of the proletariat, the Cardinal used to carry an orange that had been hollowed out and packed with a sponge made pungently odorous with savoury herbs and spices.

During the whole of the first part of the nineteenth century and during the early years of Queen Victoria's reign small decorative boxes were made and sold in great quantities to perform the same function as the Cardinal's orange. At the beginning of the century these useful and attractive little boxes were usually known as 'aromatic vinegar boxes' (we read, for instance, of the Duchess of York sending Hannah More a present of 'an elegant gold aromatic box'). By the beginning of the period in which we are principally interested they were known as 'vinaigrettes'. All busy collectors of Victoriana will come across a number of examples in the course of a year.

To be able to distinguish a vinaigrette immediately from a similar box used for (say) visiting cards or snuff, one has only to look closely at the interior. A vinaigrette would contain a piece of absorbent sponge impregnated with essential oils derived from cinnamon, cloves, lavender, mace, mint, rosemary, sage and other aromatic plants. To make these oils more volatile and therefore more effective, they would be diluted with a blend of acetic acid and alcohol. Soaked with a mixture of this kind, the piece of sponge in a vinaigrette did not have to be large to produce a potent effluvia.

To conceal this sponge and to keep it safely in place there would normally be a perforated grille—secured, usually, by the same hinge as the lid. The designers of vinaigrettes went to immense pains to make the appearance of these grilles especially attractive—the holes in them were pierced most carefully to represent flowers, leaves, birds and other decorative motifs.

The outdoor surfaces of many vinaigrettes are exquisitely engraved or chased, too, or are decorated with gems and other precious materials so that they may even be classified as jewellery. The strong acids that had to be stored in them tended to spoil all the available metals except gold. Gold vinaigrettes are therefore frequently found, and so are vinaigrettes made from porcelain, opaque white glass, clear glass and other hard materials that are not normally affected by corrosive acids.

Long before the 1851 Exhibition had become a historical memory, vinaigrettes were becoming obsolete. Their function was performed, during the rest of Queen Victoria's reign, by double-ended scent bottles, made usually of coloured glass. These bottles, which had a close-fitting stopper at each end, were intended to contain 'smelling salts' in one compartment and a pleasantly aromatic perfume in the other. They may be found today in many second-hand goods shops, and should be represented in any comprehensive collection of Victoriana.

CHAPTER FORTY-EIGHT

VALENTINES

Today hundreds of thousands of Christmas cards are bought, inscribed, posted away, received, displayed for two or three weeks and are then thrown away without too much regret. In the Victorian era the Valentine played just as important a part in the national life (in the 1870s, it was estimated, no fewer than ten thousand females were employed in the production and sale of these picturesque tokens of love and affection). Although they were never intended to be permanent keep-sakes—made, as they were, chiefly of paper and tinsel—many Victorian Valentines were so very decorative and pleasing that they have been carefully preserved.

The most attractive Victorian Valentines, to modern eyes, are those in which paper was cut, pressed and embossed to resemble the finest lace. On a Valentine framed with this delicate material, we may find bows and 'lovers' knots' made of silk ribbon, artificial flowers (or real flowers, pressed) and metal hearts, stars and other tokens. Inside this border there may be a picture or design which may have been coloured by hand. Some of the most ornate Valentines were given gilded borders, the 'gold' effect being produced with bronze powder, which was blown on to a thin imprint of varnish before the latter had dried properly.

Particularly prized by collectors are the 'trick' Valentines produced by the more ingenious designers. In these, hinged panels might open, to reveal some previously concealed scene, such as the interior of a church in which a wedding was taking place; or some part of the anatomy or clothing of a figure might be made to move amusingly by a little gentle pressure on a lever. For a short time, Valentines were produced that resembled bank-notes and postal orders (drawn, usually, on the 'Bank of Love' or some other imaginary establishment), but these were quickly suppressed.

FURTHER READING

Once you have started to collect Victoriana in earnest, you will probably feel the need for more extended information than can possibly be given in a book of this size. Here are some books that are authoritative, well-illustrated and easily obtained:

Geoffrey Bemrose, *Nineteenth Century English Pottery and Porcelain* (Faber and Faber).
Averil Colby, *Patchwork* (B. T. Batsford Ltd.).
Averil Colby, *Samplers* (B. T. Batsford Ltd.).
Ralph Edwards and L. G. G. Ramsey, *The Early Victorian Period 1830–1860* (London: The Connoisseur).
Geoffrey A. Godden, *Encyclopaedia of British Pottery and Porcelain Marks* (Herbert Jenkins).
Geoffrey A. Godden, *The Handbook of British Pottery and Porcelain Marks* (Herbert Jenkins).
Geoffrey A. Godden, *Victorian Porcelain* (Herbert Jenkins).
James Laver, *Victoriana* (Ward Lock and Co. Ltd.).
Ernest Reynolds, *Collecting Victorian Porcelain* (Arco Publications).
Amoret and Christopher Scott, *Collecting Bygones* (Max Parrish).
Hugh Wakefield, *Nineteenth Century British Glass* (Faber and Faber).
Patricia Wardle, *Victorian Silver and Silver Plate* (Herbert Jenkins).

CORGI MINI-BOOKS

All these books are available at your local bookshop or newsagent; or can be ordered direct from the publisher. Just tick the titles you want and fill in the form below.

CORGI BOOKS, Cash Sales Department, J. Barnicoat (Falmouth) Ltd., P.O. Box 11, Falmouth, Cornwall.
Please send cheque or postal order. No currency, and allow 6d. per book to cover the cost of postage and packing in U.K., 9d. per copy overseas.

NAME ....

ADDRESS ....

....